To Lindy

Christmas '93

Debrett's

COOKBOOK

'IN-A-STEW'

EASY MENUS FOR EVERY OCCASION

BY ANTOINETTE SAVILL

D1073743

HELPFUL HINTS ON WINE BY SIMON BERRY

ILLUSTRATIONS BY NICKY FIFE

Savill Trumper Publications Ltd.
- London -

Previous titles by Antoinette Savill:
Debrett's Cookbook For all Occasions
Debrett's Dinner Party Cookbook

ISBN 0-9517747-0-0

© Copyright Antoinette Savill, 1991

First published in 1991 by
Savill Trumper Publications Ltd.
64 Lexham Gardens
London W8 5JA

Distributed by Grantham Book Services
Isaac Newton Way
Alma Estate
Grantham NG31 9SD

British Library Cataloguing in Publication Data
Savill, Antoinette
    Debrett's cookbook in-a-stew easy menus for every occasion.
    I. Title II. Berry, Simon
    641.5

Typeset by Performance Publications, Billingshurst
Printed in Great Britain at Holbrook & Son Ltd., Portsmouth

To

Charlotte and Lucy
Fenella and Louise
My true friends, advisers and companions.

FOREWORD

At some time or other we have all been 'in a stew' in our own kitchen. Usually it's because we're totally disorganised due either to a complete lack of enthusiasm for cooking or to a desperate shortage of time.

Disorganisation often leads to culinary disasters mainly because we are trying to do too many things at once and end up forgetting vital ingredients or even burning them!

So, this recipe book is here to help you organise yourself, your kitchen and your menus. It provides short cuts to safe, tasty and exciting entertaining.

ACKNOWLEDGEMENTS

My thanks go first and foremost to my brother Charlie who has backed and supported me all the way; without him the book could not have been published.

I am also very grateful to Michael Colmar for his inspiration and to those special friends who helped me with vital proofing and brilliant suggestions. To Jane Sayer who typed out a totally illegible manuscript and for Hilly Trumper's unbounded enthusiasm.

I must mention Folksam International who have willingly let me experiment and perfect my recipes on their lunch guests.

A vital contribution to this book is from my sister, Nicky Fife, who has once again delighted and amused us with her brilliant cartoons.

Last, but not least, a huge thank you to Simon Berry for spending so much time choosing such delicious wines and writing about them in such an enjoyable way.

An expensive education put to the test

CONVERSION TABLES

Weights

American	Metric	Imperial
$^1/_2$ oz	10 g	$^1/_2$ oz
$^3/_4$ oz	20 g	$^3/_4$ oz
1 oz	25 g	1 oz
$^1/_4$ cup	50 g	2 oz
3 oz	75 g	3 oz
$^1/_2$ cup	125 g	4 oz
5 oz	150 g	5 oz
$^3/_4$ cup	175 g	6 oz
7 oz	200 g	7 oz
1 cup	225 g	8 oz
9 oz	250 g	9 oz
1 $^1/_4$ cup	275 g	10 oz
11 oz	300 g	11 oz
1 $^1/_2$ cup	350 g	12 oz
13 oz	375 g	13 oz
1 $^3/_4$ cup	400 g	14 oz
15 oz	425 g	15 oz
2 cups	450 g	16 oz (1 lb)
3 cups	700 g	1 $^1/_2$ lbs
4 cups	900 g	2 lbs
2 $^1/_2$ lbs	1.1 kg	2 $^1/_2$ lbs
3 lbs	1.4 kg	3 lbs
3 $^1/_2$ lbs	1.6 kg	3 $^1/_2$ lbs
4 lbs	1.8 kg	4 lbs
4 $^1/_2$ lbs	2 kg	4 $^1/_2$ lbs

Liquid Capacity

American	Metric	Imperial
1 fl.oz	25 ml	1 fl.oz
$^1/_3$ cup	50 ml	2 fl.oz
3 fl.oz	75 ml	3 fl.oz
$^1/_2$ cup	125 ml	4 fl.oz
$^2/_3$ cup	150 ml	5 fl.oz ($^1/_4$ pt)
$^3/_4$ cup	175 ml	6 fl.oz
7 fl.oz	200 ml	7 fl.oz
1 cup	225 ml	8 fl.oz
9 fl.oz	250 ml	9 fl.oz
1 $^1/_3$ cup	300 ml	10 fl.oz ($^1/_2$ pt)
2 cups	600 ml	20 fl.oz (1 pt)
1 $^1/_4$ pints	725 ml	1 $^1/_4$ pts
1 $^3/_4$ pints	1 litre	1 $^3/_4$ pts

ESSENTIALS IN MY KITCHEN CUPBOARD

Here is a list of essential goodies which I find that I need to have in my kitchen cupboard. This is a real help when you are making a quick decision as to what to cook. I hope you will find it very useful.

Things to keep in the kitchen cupboard
Bakewell paper
Balsamic vinegar
Extra virgin olive oil
Walnut oil
Pink peppercorns in brine
Cointreau
Crème de Cassis liqueur
Grand Marnier
Langdale's Essence of Rosewater
Saffron strands
Runny honey
Very good plain chocolate
Pecan nuts
Amaretti di Saronno biscuits

Things to keep in the deep freeze
Puff pastry
Shortcrust pastry
Filo pastry
Frozen spinach spheres

CONTENTS

* Extra quick and easy recipes

HELPFUL HINTS ON DRINKS PARTIES

In these days of no drink and driving, some of your wiser guests are going to drink much less alcohol, so to make them feel at ease have an exciting soft cocktail such as cranberry and grapefruit crush which is just mixing one box of grapefruit juice with one box of cranberry juice, plenty of ice and soda water. You also need to be very generous with the food, carefully organise the selection, present it imaginatively and the party will be a great success.

There is no doubt that the sound of popping champagne corks creates a great atmosphere at parties and the bubbles seem to bring out the best in people. If this is outside your budget then try some sparkling wines instead. In summer of course Pimm's No. 1 cup makes an ideal refreshing long drink which everybody enjoys.

Plan your food with care to suit your time schedule, a balance of hot and cold canapés is necessary to prevent you from becoming too rushed and not enjoying the party. My best tip for presentation is flat wickerwork baskets lined with real or fake green leaves, a few flower heads in one corner in summer or a large bundle of dried herbs in winter. Lavender or thyme being my favourite. Serve dips in real or china scallop shells with any seafood. Have all the dishes you will need for the hot food ready on the table. On a purely practical note doilies are put on them to stop the food sliding around.

If you are a non-cook or bachelor, I suggest you go to Marks and Spencer and select some of their range. Always work on the basis of:

1 or 2 preparations of fish/seafood
1 or 2 preparations of meat/poultry
1 or 2 preparations of cheese/pastry
1 or 2 preparations of vegetable/vegetarian

Here is a selection of eight recipes that I often use when I cater for drinks parties. They are all extremely popular but some of them are time consuming, so choose carefully which ones you try.

Marmite and Cheese Palmiers
Serves 50

Charlotte Farquharson, a great Marmite fan, invented this recipe. It sounds complicated but it is in fact very easy once you have made one.

Set oven at 200 C, 400 F, Gas Mark 6

> 600 g Jus-rol frozen sheets of puff pastry
> 1 small jar of Marmite
> 500 g strong Cheddar cheese, grated
> A little oil

You can make these 24 hours ahead and store in an air-tight container and warm them through before serving.

Spread the Marmite and sprinkle the cheese over two thirds of the pastry sheet. Fold the bottom third of the pastry, the bit without any cheese, over the centre third. Press the cheese very firmly in between the pastry sheet and bring the remaining third over to meet the other two thirds. Then press the edges firmly with a rolling pin all the way round and roll out to flatten a bit more. Repeat this process with each sheet of pastry until you have used all the pastry and cheese.

Now fold each strip bringing one end over to the centre and the other to meet it. Gently pinch the pastry together, slice up very thinly, then open up into traditional heart shapes and bake until crisp on oiled baking sheets. Leave lots of room for them to expand. Cool on a wire rack until needed.

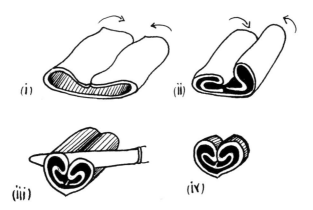

Parmesan Cheese Toasts
Serves 50

These tiny toasts make a scrumptious savoury or nibbles before dinner. You can keep them warm for a couple of hours.

Set oven at 200 C, 400 F, Gas Mark 6

> 1 large loaf of sliced white bread
> 250 g mayonnaise
> 250 g Parmesan cheese
> Salt and black pepper
> 1 tablespoon Worcestershire sauce
> Few drops Tabasco

Remove the crusts from the bread and cut out eighty small circles. Mix all the remaining ingredients together and keep chilled for at least one hour. Lightly toast the bread on both sides and then spoon the mixture onto each round. Put them in the oven for about five minutes until puffed up and golden.

You can also add finely chopped anchovies to the mixture as a change from time to time.

Cocktail Sausages in Honey and Tarragon
Serves 50

Everybody's favourite, these sausages are sweet and sticky so make sure you serve them with a bundle of cocktail sticks in a little jar.

> 2.3 kg miniature cocktail sausages
> 900 g jar runny honey
> 1 large bunch fresh tarragon
> A little oil

Half cook the sausages in two batches in roasting tins. Mix a little oil with them to stop them sticking to the pan. Add the honey and tarragon leaves and return to the oven and cook until crunchy and sticky. They keep warm for ages.

Water Chestnuts Wrapped in Bacon
Serves 50

3 tins water chestnuts, drained
1 kg rindless streaky bacon
Soy sauce
Cocktail sticks

Wrap each chestnut in suitably sized pieces of bacon, sprinkle with a little soy sauce. Cook in batches under the grill until crispy turning once only. Serve on a warm plate with cocktail sticks already in them.

This is an excellent savoury too.

Savoury for 12

1 tin water chestnuts, drained
225 g rindless streaky bacon
Soy sauce

Gravad Lax and Dill Sauce Canapés
Serves 50

A slightly more exotic idea than smoked salmon on brown bread and butter and a lot less expensive too.

2 x 225 g packets of Gravad Lax
1 jar of 175 g prepared dill sauce, from any delicatessen
3 x 250 g packets of cocktail pumpernickel rounds

Cut each round of pumpernickel in half and spread with the dill sauce and a twist of Gravad Lax. Arrange on a plate, decorate and keep chilled until ready to serve.

Poppy Seed Prawns and Chilli Dip

Serves 50

Of all my cocktail party eats these are, without fail, the most popular probably because they are so unusual. Unfortunately they are the most time consuming as well.

Set oven at 200 C, 400 F, Gas Mark 6

> 1.5 kg fresh prawns in shells
> 2 boxes 450 g Jus-rol frozen filo pastry sheets
> Sunflower oil
> 1 jar poppy seeds
> 2 jars Sainsbury's tomato and chilli relish

Take the heads and shells off the prawns leaving the tail on. Wrap each one in a double strip of filo pastry and brush with oil so the pastry sticks together and place on a big oiled baking tray. When the tray is full, sprinkle with poppy seeds and bake for five to ten minutes until crispy. Serve warm with a little pot of the tomato and chilli relish.

Chicken Sesame Seed Goujons with Sweet and Sour Sauce
Serves 50

The great thing about these goujons is that you can make them the day before and refrigerate them. Heat them in a very hot oven just before serving.

Set oven at 200 C, 400 F, Gas Mark 6

12 large chicken suprêmes
3 eggs
150 ml milk
450 g plain flour
$^3/_4$ teaspoon salt
1 teaspoon cayenne pepper
75 g sesame seeds
Vegetable oil for frying
3 x 160 g jars Sharwood's stir fry sweet and sour sauce

Slice the chicken across into thin strips. Beat the eggs with the milk in a large bowl, mix together with the chicken pieces. Place the flour, salt, cayenne pepper and sesame seeds in a separate bowl and toss the chicken until well coated. You can leave the chicken at this stage until just before the party.

Warm the sauce in a saucepan with a tiny bit of water. Pour oil into a deep saucepan or frying pan and heat until the point when the chicken strips rise to the surface, brown and crispy. Turn the goujons over for a minute and then lift out and drain on absorbent kitchen paper. Keep warm until needed, serve with a bundle of cocktail sticks and a bowl of sauce.

Mini Spinach and Cream Cheese Roulades
Serves 50

You can make these 24 hours ahead of time which is good news when you have got so much to do at the last minute.

Set oven at 200 C, 400 F, Gas Mark 6

> 907 g frozen chopped spinach spheres
> Salt, pepper and nutmeg
> 50 g butter
> 12 eggs, separated
> 50 g grated Parmesan cheese
> 450 g cream cheese
> 75 g fresh chives
> 11 g gelatine
> 225 g Greek strained yoghurt
> Parsley, flowers or quails eggs to decorate

Line three roulade tins or two big roasting tins with Bakewell paper. Thaw the spinach and cook over medium heat with very little water. Drain and return to a big non-stick saucepan and heat through. Add the seasoning to taste, the butter and all the egg yolks and mix well. In a big bowl whisk the egg whites until stiff and fold into the spinach. Carefully pour into the tins. Bake immediately until firm to touch, about 10-15 minutes.

Lay out three pieces of greaseproof paper onto your table and sprinkle with grated Parmesan cheese. Turn the roulades onto each one, divide each roulade into three sections and roll up each section using up all the Bakewell paper. Leave the mini roulades to cool for half an hour or so.

Dissolve the gelatine as instructed on the packet and mix with the cream cheese, yoghurt and chives. Season to taste with salt and pepper. Chill the mixture until it is very thick and then spread over the inside of the roulades. Trim the ends and wrap up firmly in clingfilm or foil and chill for up to 24 hours. You will end up with nine mini roulades and you can cut each one into about ten slices.

Serve the sliced up roulades displayed on large plates with fresh parsley, flowers or quails eggs, according to how imaginative you feel.

Wines for parties

Wine at a drinks party has to perform one vital function - to keep the conversation going. Don't worry unduly, as you might at a dinner party, that nobody actually mentions the wine they are drinking - that's not what it's there for. If the conversation centres around how delicious the wine is, you've probably spent twice as much on it than was strictly necessary. Equally, you certainly don't want people to be talking about how filthy the wine is - either at the party or when they ring each other up to discuss it through their hangovers the next day. So the trick is to find a middle course.

White wine is always more popular than red, but resist the temptation to get anything too dry. I know that the popular convention is that The Sophisticated only like dry wine, and I am sure that you and your guests are nothing if not Sophisticated, but this convention mainly applies to wine with food. The race that invented the concept of wine **without** food was the Germans. They drink beer with their food, probably to disguise how unappetising their food tastes, and drink wines throughout the day much as we drink coffee or, indeed, beer. This is a very civilised habit, and we, The Sophisticated, would do well to adopt it. As a result, there is a wide range of German wines that are low in alcohol (sometimes 9% compared with 12 or 13% for French white wines, which really makes a difference if the conversation is to remain coherent), dry enough not to offend The Ultra Sophisticated, and sweet enough to satisfy the Unsophisticated who may have wandered in without your noticing. They actually taste of grapes - a rare quality, if we are to believe the majority of our Wine Writers. Furthermore, they are remarkably good value for money, having been pooh-poohed for so long by The Sophisticated Rich.

I am not talking about the supermarket blends - the Liebfraumilchs and the Eine Kleine Nacht Musiks that have been responsible for the decline of Germany's reputation as a wine producing nation. Look for wines from single vineyards from the Rhine or the Moselle, and expect to pay between £3.50 and £6.00 a bottle. German wine labels are very confusing at first, but actually very logical and informative once you have cracked the code. Moselles come in green bottles, Rhine wines (Hocks to the traditional) in brown bottles, which is an easy start. Single vineyards are also instantly recognisable - they are mainly given two names, the first being the name of the village they belong to, which will always end in the letters 'er' (German for 'of'), the second being the name of the vineyard. Traben-Trarbacher Würzgarten, therefore, is the Würzgarten (literally 'Spice Garden' which sounds much friendlier) vineyard of Traben-Trarbach - and if you can master that one the rest of the wines of Germany will seem dead simple. The name of the grape will also feature prominently, which is considerate - Riesling or Sylvaner/Müller-Thurgau are two safe bets. Finally, look for the magic words 'Kabinett', or 'Qualitätswein', which will tell you that the wine is about the right level of dryness for your party, and not one of the sweeter, utterly delicious pudding wines which Germany also produces. The very, very good news is that, as a rough rule of thumb, the drier the German wine, the lower the price.

If you think you should have some red wine as well, choose something fruity and light and uncomplicated. Beaujolais is perfect - it was once described to me, by a very serious Burgundian Négociant, as 'wine you don't have to think about', which suits a drinks party down to the ground. Please, however, avoid the over-rated Beaujolais Nouveau at all costs.

You may well feel that you need to have some fizz at your party, especially if you are celebrating something. Champagne is, of course, the best, but really the same rules apply - don't go madly extravagant. There are some excellent own label champagnes on the market, especially from the more traditional wine merchants, at prices lower or similar to the famous 'Grandes Marques', as well as some first class champagnes from lesser known companies, such as Gosset and Canard Duchène. But beware. By and large, you get what you pay for with champagne, and there is no doubt that the cheapest champagnes are very much nastier than the equivalent-priced Sparkling Wines from elsewhere in the world. And we've all suffered from the after effects of nasty champagne enough to try not to inflict the same experience on our friends.

Luckily, there has been a revolution in the past few years that has seen a dramatic rise in quality in Sparkling Wine. Certainly if you intend to mix the fizz with any other ingredient - orange juice, Guinness, or brandy, a sugar lump and Angostura Bitters, it is a waste to use real champagne. The reason champagne is so popular at celebrations is that the cork goes pop in a satisfactory manner, and that the alcohol is carried to the system faster by the bubbles. Both these functions are performed equally well by Sparkling Wine, probably at half the cost, and now without a noticeable decline in quality.

Finally a word about quantities. You know the capacity of your friends better than I do, but half a bottle a head is the norm, especially if there are a few non drinkers and people have to drive home afterwards. Order a little more than this, because it is always embarrassing if the drink runs out and your guests turn ugly. Many good wine merchants will let you have the wine on a 'Sale or Return' basis, but ask before you order, and don't put anything on ice that you want them to take back, as the labels are liable to wash off.

ORGANISING BUSINESS LUNCHES AND DINNERS

The most important thing, of course, is to find out the likes and dislikes of each of your guests. Choose a menu that reflects the importance of the occasion as well as fitting your budget and your ability to produce the meal. The ideal menu is one that allows you to do all the preparations in advance so that you are free to entertain your clients or guests. If you are a really nervous cook try out the menu first, an important occasion is not a good time for experimenting! Always avoid seafood and offal in case of embarrassing allergies and avoid food that is difficult or messy to eat. I also suggest that you have the starter on the table when your guests walk into the room as first impressions are the most important. Prepare everything possible in advance including the vegetables as this minimises the chances of a steamy kitchen and a steamy cook!

Lunches, except Sunday lunch of course, tend to be less smart, so do make sure you serve lighter dishes so that guests can go on to their appointments for the day and not fall asleep for the rest of the afternoon. I have to choose the wines for my directors' lunches every day so I go by instinct and experience rather than actual knowledge but so far I seem to have sniffed out all the right ones. My rules are very simple, I take into consideration first the importance of the lunch or dinner and choose a wine in the relative price range this narrows you down to certain vintages, châteaux and house wines. Then of course you must complement your food with the wines and not detract from the flavours or overwhelm them. Don't forget at lunches people generally like to keep their wits about them so lighter wines are preferred. If you are serving both white and then red wines at the party make sure they complement each other, don't get a really cheap one and contrast it with a very expensive one, everyone will notice and won't be impressed. Always remember some people dislike either red or white so do make sure you have an emergency supply of each and plenty of fizzy water.

I will just say that I think it is a complete fallacy that men don't like puddings, their faces light up as soon as they see a gooey chocolate or nursery pudding probably because they don't get them at home. So I always offer a dessert at business lunches or dinners. My suggestion is that you also cater for those who would prefer cheese and fruit by carefully organising a very good selection and display of both. Always end the meal with a choice of freshly ground or decaffeinated coffee or tea and chocolates or mints depending on the sort of pudding you offered.

WINTER MENU FOR SIX

    Creamy goat's cheese mousse
      and tomato vinaigrette
* Wild duck with kumquats
      Cointreau and marmalade sauce
* Sesame seed roast potatoes
    Celeriac purée
    Chocolate and coffee bean
      gâteau

Wine:
    Red Loire, 1987 Chinon,
      Clos des Varennes, Joguet
    Red Rhône, 1983 Hermitage

SUMMER MENU FOR TEN

* Chilled asparagus in Parma
      Ham with pear sauce
    Fillets of salmon in fennel
      cream sauce
* Crispy fried fennel
    New potatoes
    My tarte au citron

    Chablis, 1987 Mont de Milieu,
      Premier Cru, J.C. Dauvissat
    White Burgundy, 1988 Meursault,
      Charles Viénot

Creamy Goat's Cheese Mousse and Tomato Vinaigrette

Serves 6

Goat's cheese has become very trendy, not everybody likes it though so do be sure of it's popularity before you present your guests with a starter like this.

Half 397 g tin chopped tomatoes with herbs
$^1/_2$ teaspoon sugar
150 ml walnut oil vinaigrette (page 81)
200 g pitted, black olives
300 g fresh soft goat's cheese
11 g gelatine
Salt and pepper
300 ml cream, whipped
A few cherry tomatoes and fresh basil leaves for decoration

Line six ramekins with circles of Bakewell paper.

First mix the tomatoes and sugar with the vinaigrette, give it a good stir and chill until needed. Dissolve the gelatine as instructed on the packet. Mash the cheese with the gelatine and season to taste. Fold in the whipped cream and pour into the ramekins. Cover with clingfilm and chill until set.

Chop the olives up very finely in a food processor and keep on a saucer.

Turn out the mousses onto the centre of each plate and spoon the vinaigrette around them and decorate with a few halved cherry tomatoes and whole fresh basil leaves. Now spoon the chopped olives all over the tops of the mousses, carefully spreading it so it doesn't fall over the edges. The contrast looks fabulous.

This is particularly good with walnut or other savoury breads and unsalted butter.

Wild Duck with Kumquats, Cointreau and Marmalade Sauce

Serves 6

Marmalade makes a good short cut for sauces which is why I have used it a couple of times in my cookbook.

Set oven at 200 C, 400 F, Gas Mark 6

> 3 wild duck
> 3 tablespoons olive oil
> 3 branches thyme
> Salt and pepper
> 225 g kumquats
> 5 tablespoons Tiptree Fine Cut Orange marmalade
> 50 g pecan nuts
> Juice from 2 large oranges
> 4 tablespoons Cointreau

Put one tablespoon of oil in a roasting tin and spoon the rest over the birds. Season them with salt, pepper and thyme and roast in the oven for 20 minutes and then take them out to make the sauce.

Blanch the kumquats in boiling water for four minutes. Drain and refresh under cold water. Drain off any excess fat in the roasting tin and smear the ducks with most of the marmalade and fill the cavities with the rest. Scatter the pecans over the ducks, pour the orange juice into the tin and return to the oven for a further 15 minutes.

Remove the ducks from the pan and set on a carving board to rest. This allows the meat to settle before carving.

Now scrape round the roasting tin on a hob and bring the sauce to boiling point. Stir in the Cointreau, adjust seasoning and simmer for a few minutes. Carve ducks and present them in an attractive fan shape on each plate with a crispy leg. Pour the sauce around the base of the duck and over the leg and serve immediately.

Sesame Seed Roast Potatoes
Serves 6

You can par-boil the potatoes well in advance and keep covered or chilled until needed.

1 kg potatoes, peeled and quartered
2 tablespoons olive oil
2 tablespoons sunflower oil
2 tablespoons walnut oil
1 tablespoon of sesame seeds

Par-boil the potatoes and drain. Put the oils together in a frying pan and sauté the potatoes until crisp. Drain on absorbent paper. Pour out nearly all the oil from the frying pan and quickly sauté the sesame seeds until golden. Put the potatoes in a warm dish. Drain the sesame seeds on more paper, sprinkle them over the potatoes and serve.

Crispy Fried Fennel
Serves 5

You can double up the recipe for a party of ten. I use this recipe to accompany grilled salmon or the fillets of salmon in fennel cream sauce (page 28).

4 large bulbs of fennel
Olive oil
Salt and pepper

Trim the fennel and slice into rings. Boil in salted water until crunchy but cooked. Drain and rinse in cold water. Heat some oil in a frying pan and fry the fennel pieces, season with salt and pepper. Drain on absorbent kitchen paper and serve immediately.

Celeriac Purée
Serve 8

Celeriac on its own is an acquired taste, made up like this, however, even the most unadventurous palates enjoy it.

Set oven at 200 C, 400 F, Gas Mark 6

> 1 large celeriac
> 750 g old potatoes, peeled and cubed
> 75 g butter
> 2 tablespoons vinegar
> Juice of 1 lemon
> Salt, pepper and nutmeg
> 200 ml single cream
> Extra butter and cayenne pepper

Cook the potatoes, drain and mash. Then slice off the celeriac roots and the skin, cut into cubes and boil in water with the two tablespoons of vinegar to prevent browning. As soon as the celeriac is soft drain and mash it with the potatoes, butter and cream. Season to taste with salt, pepper and nutmeg and add lemon juice.

When I am ready to re-heat the purée, I usually transfer it into an ovenproof dish and dot with extra butter or a little cayenne pepper and bake for about 20 minutes until golden brown.

Chocolate and Coffee Bean Gâteau
Serves 12

The combination of chocolate and coffee cream is fatal, a double dose of cholesterol and caffeine, definitely heart attack stuff!

Set oven at 190 C, 375 F, Gas Mark 5

A little melted butter and Bakewell paper
150 g plain chocolate
125 g unsalted butter
100 g caster sugar
100 g ground almonds
4 eggs, separated
50 g fresh brown breadcrumbs
2 tablespoons melted raspberry jam
450 ml double cream
100 g icing sugar, sifted
2 teaspoons instant coffee, dissolved in 2 teaspoons boiling water
12 coffee beans

Line the base of a spring release tin with Bakewell paper and brush with the melted butter. Stir the chocolate over very low heat until melted. Remove from the heat. Cream the butter and sugar until light and fluffy. Stir in the almonds, egg yolks, breadcrumbs and chocolate.

Stiffly beat the egg whites and fold into the mixture. Pour into the tin and bake for 30 - 35 minutes until firm to touch. Leave to cool under a damp, clean cloth. Turn out the cake onto a wire rack and brush the cake with the jam. Whip the cream and fold in the icing sugar and coffee and spread all over the cake and decorate with the coffee beans.

Keep chilled until needed.

Chilled Asparagus in Parma Ham with Pear Sauce

Serves 10

You can't make this recipe the day before because the pear sauce will go brown. Anyway it's so quick and easy you don't really need to.

> 40 spears of asparagus
> Salt and pepper
> 10 slices Parma ham
> 4 ripe pears, peeled and cored
> 2 ^{1}/$_2$ tablespoons lemon juice
> Chives for decoration

Cut the asparagus spears into half and discard the tough stems, cook the tips in salted boiling water until al dente. Drain and refresh under cold water and dry on absorbent paper until completely cold. Wrap bundles of four asparagus tips in a piece of ham and place in the middle of a plate. Liquidize the pears with the lemon juice and enough water to make a spooning consistency. Season with a touch of black pepper and spoon around the parcel of asparagus. Decorate the plate with a few small criss-crosses of chives and chill until needed.

Fillets of Salmon in Fennel Cream Sauce
Serves 10

Set oven at 190 C, 375 F, Gas Mark 5

2 ^{1}/$_2$ kg fresh salmon, to be gutted
1 large handful fresh dill
700 ml strong fish stock
200 ml cream
100 g butter
3 large fennel bulbs, trimmed
Salt and pepper
2 tablespoons of plain flour
200 ml dry white wine

To make a good fish stock, ask your fishmonger for some fish bones, heads and tails. Sole is best. Put them in a large saucepan with an onion studded with cloves, a bay leaf, a sprig of thyme, salt and pepper and cover with water. Boil until reduced by half. Top up with white wine and reduce to half again. Sieve the stock carefully to make sure no little bones have slipped through and proceed with the sauce.

First wash and dry the salmon. Then slice the fennel finely and cook gently in the butter until soft but not brown. Meanwhile, fillet the salmon into ten neat pieces and lay them in a buttered oven proof dish. Season with salt and pepper and leave for a few moments.

Now stir the flour into the fennel and then incorporate the wine, stock and cream in that order. When the sauce is thick and glossy leave to cool slightly before liquidizing. Sieve the sauce into a bowl and correct the seasoning. Pour the sauce over the salmon fillets, cover with foil and bake for 15 minutes. Serve as soon as possible with the crispy fried fennel (page 24).

My Tarte au Citron

Serves 10

Tarte au Citron is hardly ever served in England which is a great shame as it is a very refreshing dessert which traditionally is served without cream.

Set oven at 190 C, Gas Mark 5

> 500 g packet fresh shortcrust pastry
> 4 eggs
> 175 g sugar
> 150 ml lemon juice
> 100 ml orange juice
> Grated zest of 1 lemon
> 50 g butter
> 4 tablespoons double cream
> 1 lemon to decorate
> Icing sugar for dusting

Roll out the pastry and line a large fluted flan tin with a removable base. Prick the bottom of the pastry with a fork, line with greaseproof paper and bake blind filled with dried beans or ceramic balls for 15 minutes or until light brown. Take out paper and beans and cool.

To make filling; place eggs, sugar, lemon and orange juice and zest in a bowl and whisk together. Melt the butter with the cream and whisk in a large saucepan over low heat. Add the egg mixture and continue cooking, stirring all the time, until it thickens. Pour the custard into the pastry case and bake for 20 minutes. Cool the tart before lifting out of the tin and sliding it off the base onto a serving dish. Cut very thin slices of lemon and use them to decorate the flan and dust with icing sugar before serving.

Choosing Wine for Dinner Parties

If you are going to the time and trouble and expense of organising a dinner party, you do not want to jeopardise everything by allowing your guests to bring along the wine. Matching food with wine is a very delicate science, and you are hardly likely to ring your friends a week before and tell them exactly what you are cooking and what they should bring along to go with it. More likely they will each bring whatever they find lurking in the kitchen, or make a last minute dash to the late night off-licence, and hope that somebody else has been more thoughtful and generous. You will end up with five or six different bottles, each one slightly nastier than the one before, with the exception of the bottle of delicious Sancerre, brought by mistake.

Far better to make it perfectly clear to all your guests that you will be providing the food and the wine, and that you are only able to perform this feat of unparalleled generosity on the understanding that you will never be expected to bring a bottle back to them. If they really come out in spots at the thought of not bringing something to help the party go with a swing, let them bring chocolates, or flowers, or the marching band of the Coldstream Guards. But please, please look after the food and the wine yourself.

Start young and get older, start light and get heavier, start cheap and get more expensive. Exactly the sort of advice Nanny might have given you about Life in General, but it works with wines as well. Never try to follow an expensive mature Claret with a cheaper younger one, hoping that by that stage people won't notice. They will. Your palate gets very used to being spoiled very quickly, and the second wine will taste thin and disappointing in comparison, although it would probably have been perfectly alright if it had been served first. Equally light, dry white wines are delicious at the beginning of a meal but really cannot hope to compete if they are sandwiched between heavier reds.

Decant your red wines. All of them, not just the oldest and rarest. It is a common fallacy that decanting simply separates wine from its sediment, and that decanting is only necessary - desirable even - with older, finer wines that have been laid down until a noticeable sediment forms. Decanting allows oxygen to get at the wine, and oxygen is what allows wine to mature - the youngest and rawest wines, therefore, benefit most from the process, and can stand being decanted at least an hour or two before the meal. If you don't have a decanter, pour the wine into a jug, wash out the bottle, and pour the wine back - the difference will amaze you. But if you do have a decanter, use it - it is one of the easiest ways to turn an ordinary supper into a special dinner party.

Wines for Fish, Poultry and Veal

The delicacy of white meat, whether fish or fowl, is the most important consideration here. Naturally enough, the best wines to complement the subtle flavours are delicate themselves. Don't think that this restricts your choice, though - the world is full of delicate wines, both red and white, of sufficient variety to keep you experimenting for years.

The white Sauvignon grape makes wines which often fit the bill perfectly. Fresh, light and very refreshing, they tend to have a very attractive smell of grass or sometimes gooseberries. The acidity they have is a good thing, especially if you need to cut through a creamy sauce.

The most famous - and consequently the most expensive - come from the Loire, especially Sancerre and Pouilly. Don't confuse Pouilly in the Loire with Pouilly-Fuissé in Burgundy, even though the wine made from the Sauvignon across the river from Sancerre is called, with typical Gallic clarity, Pouilly-Fumé. If you are still confused stick to the Sauvignons from Ménétou-Salon, slightly further to the east, slightly less well-known, and therefore slightly less expensive. Or try the dry white Sauvignons from Bordeaux. There is a very curious gap in the hierarchy of these wines. A handful - Domaine de Chevalier, Ch. Laville-Haut Brion, and Ch. Carbonnieux for example - have always been highly prized and highly priced. But the Bordelais have only recently rediscovered their capacity for making delicious dry white wines at all price levels, with the result that many little-known châteaux to the south of the city are producing some of the best value Sauvignons in France.

Outside France, look for the Sauvignons from Australia and especially New Zealand. Sometimes, just to keep us on our toes, they take a leaf from the book of those nice people from Pouilly and refer to the grape as the Fumé Blanc. Pay no attention and drink it up anyway - it's still delicious.

The Chardonnay grape produces richer, rounder white wines, at their best when aged for a while in oak casks. Very often they can overwhelm simply cooked fish, but are excellent with poultry. Burgundy is the home of this grape, and the wines from the world famous villages of the Côte d'Or - Meursault and Puligny-Montrachet, for example - are universally acknowledged to be some of the finest white wines known to man. Other countries have tried to copy this success. North East Italy produces some excellent, reasonably priced alternatives, and the Western States of America, specifically California and Washington, are capable of making some real stunners. Australia and Chile can also produce fine Chardonnay, although the flavours tend to be even more intense and may be too powerful for some tastes.

For the perfect Chardonnay / food combination, however, you must go back to Burgundy, and a curious quirk of nature. The chalk soil of Chablis was formed millions of years ago when the area was, believe it or not, next to the sea. The vineyards lie on ancient oyster beds, and produce wines which are, appropriately enough, superb with oysters and other shellfish.

However, don't feel bound to stick to white wines - even with fish dishes. There are plenty of red wines, usually from the more northerly vineyards, that are light and elegant. Try the Loire reds from Chinon and Bourgueil, especially with heavier fish like salmon, and veal dishes.

Again, experiment and remember. One of the best meals I have had in my life was in a curious bar on the banks of the estuary of the Guadalquivir in Andalucia - freshly caught red mullet and ice cold Manzanilla Sherry. Perfectly normal to the people of Jerez, but a stunning combination to the world-weary palates you might be entertaining.

Wines for Game, Meat and Offal

In exactly the same way that it was possible to define the best wines for white meat by the grape variety they come from, so is it with wines for red meat. Although you and I would find it very difficult to tell the difference between these grapes on the vine, the variations in taste that they produce are striking.

The Cabernet Sauvignon is the classic grape of Bordeaux, and is usually blended there with a proportion of juice from the Merlot grape. This is to stop it from becoming too dour and rigid, for it is an upright, aristocratic grape, rather too proud of its ancestry but admirably noble nevertheless and - its great strength - capable of aging for many years until it achieves a soft mellowness. The Merlot is altogether more attractive and fruity when young, but lacks the staying power of its usual companion. Together, therefore, they make wonderful, harmonious wines, that go beautifully with plainly cooked meats - not for nothing is Red Bordeaux, or Claret, known as 'The Englishman's Wine'.

Elsewhere in the world, hardly surprisingly, this combination has been imitated, even though the Cabernet Sauvignon seems to lose some of its hautiness when 'abroad' and is often found, very satisfactorily, on its own in countries like Australia, Bulgaria and Chile.

The other really 'First Division' grape variety is the Pinot Noir. Much more temperamental and difficult to grow than the Cabernet Sauvignon, it only really reaches its full potential in Burgundy and, some would say, only there in the handful of villages that make up the Côte d'Or. But you have to be richer and richer to enjoy the very best Côte d'Or burgundies. Luckily the wines of the Mâconnais and Châlonnais to the south are rapidly gaining in quality, and there is some indication that Northern Italy, California and New Zealand will soon be able to offer a wider variety of excellent alternatives to red burgundy. The world is certainly crying out for this. About fifteen years ago, Burgundy used to be excellent value, and as common a sight on our dining tables as Claret is today. Superb with game of all types, it was satisfying red wine that was clearly made by people who took their mealtimes very seriously. The great red wines of the Northern Rhône, highly prized a hundred years ago, are now greatly neglected, despite being some of the best value wines in the world. When was the last time you bought an Hermitage, or a Côte Rôtie? The Syrah grape, which is solely responsible for these wonderful wines, deserves to be mentioned in the same breath as Pinot Noir and Cabernet Sauvignon. Once again it is the wine makers of the 'New World' who are exploiting it to its full potential, but as they tend to refer to it as 'Shiraz' it is doubtful that their success will affect the makers of Rhône wine to any great extent. Shiraz or Syrah, Hermitage or Hunter Valley, these wines are beefy, masculine drinks, perfect with richer stews or, indeed, any warming winter dish you can think of.

I may have mentioned the three essential red wine grapes, and en passant two others - Cabernet Franc for the Loire reds and Gamay for Beaujolais - but the styles of red wines are much more disparate than those of white wines. There has been no space to list the regional grapes of France, which, with modern wine making techniques, are becoming worthy rivals to the classics as opposed to mere country cousins. Equally, Italy's indigenous varieties such as the Sangiovese and the Nebbiolo cannot be ignored when it comes to choosing wines to accompany Italian food. Zinfandel, Cinsault, Tempranillo and Carignan are all varieties which are growing more and more popular in their own right, and which have their own individual characteristics that make them suitable for different dishes.

Pudding Wines

Once upon a time, you were civilized if you cooked your food before you ate it. A little later, you were civilized if you drank wine with your food. Now the real mark of civilisation is to drink pudding wine with your puddings.

This is a Thoroughly Good Thing. First of all, sweeter wines tend to be lighter in alcohol, which is a wise way of ending an evening if anyone is driving home. (But please note that some wines are sweet because their fermentation has been stopped by the addition of locally produced brandy - Port, Madeira and Muscat de Beaumes de Venise, for example - and therefore do not apply.) Secondly, they are delicious. And thirdly they are ridiculously cheap.

You may not feel that this last statement is true if you have just raided your piggy bank for a bottle or two of Château d'Yquem at somewhere around £150 a go. But not all pudding wines cost as much as Yquem - in fact the vast majority will cost you less than a tenth of the price. £15 may still seem fairly steep for one bottle; probably far more than you will spend on other bottles for the same dinner party. But pudding wine is absurdly expensive to make. The grapes that go into making it are usually extremely concentrated, and have to be picked individually by vineyard workers who have to be highly trained. In order to reach this ripeness the vines are left unpicked until late in the year - a very risky business that often leads to the entire crop being ruined by frost. Furthermore, a single vine in Sauternes will only produce a glass of wine, compared to a litre of wine from each vine in, say, the Médoc. Taking all these factors into consideration, it is a miracle that any pudding wine costs less than £150 a bottle. And when you consider that you can easily share one bottle between eight guests, you will I hope realise that, as bench-marks of civilization go, pudding wine is a great bargain.

The most expensive come, not surprisingly, from the parishes around Yquem: Sauternes and Barsac. There is no need to spend more than £25 to get a wine that is very nearly as good as the ultimate - Ch. Coutet, for example, or Lafaurie-Peyraguey or Rieussec. For excellent value for money look across the opposite bank of the Garonne to Ste. Croix du Mont.

Vouvray, in the Loire, makes extraordinary sweet wines that have the potential to last for decades and become more and more subtle and fascinating as they do so. Look for the word 'Moelleux' on the label, because the same producers also produce dry and medium dry wines from the same grapes. Equally the late harvested wines of Alsace, the Rhône and even the Pyrenées are beginning to be seen on more and more lists.

Australia is also producing some excellent dessert wines, often from what they brazenly refer to as the 'Rhine Riesling' grape, but sometimes from such exotic combinations as Orange Muscat and Flora. These can be superb, with rich, concentrated flavours that seem to stay in the mouth for ever. They are also reviving the habit of bottling these wines in half bottles, something the Europeans have been reluctant to do but which is a very welcome move; a half bottle is really enough for six relatively abstemious people.

But Germany, where the whole process was probably invented, makes some of the most undervalued sweet white wines of all. Find, if you can, some of the Auslesen or Trockenbeerenauslesen wines from the Rhine or the Moselle - or, if you're really lucky, some Eiswein, when the grapes are picked in late November when they have just been frozen. Your guests, and your taste buds, will love you for the rest of your life.

Presentation of Cheeses, Breads and Fruit

I enjoy imaginative presentation and once I started to use life-like silk leaves to arrange in my selection of wickerwork flat trays or baskets nothing seemed to compare, so I raided the garden for vine leaves or similar greenery and lined the baskets with them before arranging the cheeses on top. Choose three or four cheeses, all different shapes, textures, colours and sizes. The bigger the tray you use the more noticeable the display. In the summer you can add a few pretty flowers, bunches of dried herbs or lavender in winter. You can use bunches of fresh black or redcurrants which contrast beautifully with the cheeses. Here is a guide to choosing cheeses: have one goat's cheese log, one blue cheese, soft or hard. One wedge of a coloured rind cheese and a whole small cheese, like a camembert.

Be very organised and place the cheese plates, butter and baskets full of chunky wedges of different types of bread with the cheese board on a separate table with a pretty cloth, this makes a feature of it at the party as well as being ready to serve. Be adventurous and buy different breads, Harrods, Clarkes of Kensington, Cranks and Justin de Blank all make delicious varieties like pumpkin, onion, herb and walnut. Sainsbury's and Marks and Spencer both make good breads like Roggenbrot, Panne Di Olive and Tarallodi Noci. Cut these up into wedges and mix with exciting rolls or french sticks.

The art of presenting fresh fruit as an alternative to a pudding is to make it so tempting that your guests will feel that you have made a special effort for them. Be organised, choose your fruit well in advance so that it is perfectly ripe, there is nothing more disappointing than a rock hard peach or nectarine. In summer I decorate my display of fruit with some fresh strawberries or lychees and in winter I find that fresh dates and kumquats look marvellous. You can use your fruit display on a china or glass stand as an alternative to a flower arrangement which saves even more time, effort and money. When I do this I often use one fruit only for example a pile of fresh figs on vine leaves in summer or clementines piled high with little sprigs of holly in winter.

ARRANGING THEME PARTIES WITH MENUS

My best advice to you is to try not to be too ambitious. If you have a full time job and get home at 6 or 7 pm it is a good idea to keep the numbers down so that you are not too exhausted to enjoy the evening yourself. Now is your chance to really indulge yourself. Pick your theme for your party and start building up ideas. The more you put into it the more sensational it will be. Helium balloons in all shapes and sizes are great fun and you can go mad on the table decorations. I have given you some ideas with each theme and hope that you have great fun in trying them out.

Plan your parties meticulously, make a check list of all you need as well as your shopping list. When you have chosen your menu, check that you have enough plates there is nothing worse than realising at the last minute that you have used the pudding plates for the starter. Check your menu to see that you haven't included a particular food that someone is allergic to and that you have enough glasses, napkins, cutlery, chairs, cloths etc. It is such a relief to know that there is nothing last minute to do except take the dishes out of the oven or hot plate. So get any messy and noisy frying, whisking, grinding of coffee beans done before your guests arrive and if your kitchen is clean and organised you are half way there. Make plenty of ice cubes and keep them in polythene bags in the freezer and have all the suitable wines and champagnes chilled and the red wines opened and at room temperature so that you can really relax before your guests arrive.

If I know that I am going to be in a real rush I lay the table the night before. Place cards are a brilliant idea because you will inevitably be organising food in the kitchen or serving drinks to your guests and your well thought out seating plan may be forgotten at the last minute. Do include flowers on your shopping list. A small vase of flowers on the dining room table makes all the difference. You can buy ready made up fresh or dried arrangements so easily but do remember, don't have a huge tall arrangement in the centre of the table or your guests won't be able to see each other.

Valentine's Day

ST. VALENTINE'S DINNER FOR SIX

Indulge all your romantic dreams, cover the table with a lovely white cloth, red roses, red and gold napkins and candles. Godiva make wonderful gold covered chocolate hearts or if this is too much then go for a pink and gold combination. You could then have pink champagne with little canapés to start. Dim the lights, put the slushy music on and go and wallow in a bubble bath before everyone arrives.

MENU

Smoked salmon and pink peppercorn roulade

* Roast mallard with cinnamon and cloves
* Creamed potatoes
* Baby sweetcorn and Parisienne carrots in chive butter

Valentine hearts with blackcurrant coulis

You can do all the shopping and lay the table the day before and then start by making the roulade then the creamed potatoes and lastly the pudding and refrigerate them until the following evening. So that on the night all you have to do is to cook the duck, reheat the potatoes, cook the vegetables and lastly unwrap the roulade, slice up and decorate, unmould the hearts onto plates and pour the coulis around. Keep away from direct heat if you can't return them to the fridge.

Wine: *Alsace, 1988 Riesling Schoenenbourg, R. Schmidt*
            Rhône, 1985 Côte Rôtie
            White Bordeaux, 1986 Ch. de Malle, Sauternes

Smoked Salmon and
Pink Peppercorn Roulade

Serves 6

An all time classic which I produce at almost every Directors' lunch and dinner party. You can't fail to impress.

450 g sliced best smoked salmon
11 g sachet gelatine, dissolved as instructed
Salt and pepper
1 tablespoon pink peppercorns in brine
450 g Greek strained yoghurt
Little rosettes of tomato skins and sprigs of parsley

Lay out the sliced salmon on a large sheet of clingfilm or greaseproof paper. Make sure there are no gaps and that you have a neat rectangle. Trim the edges if necessary.

In a mixing bowl blend the gelatine with the salt and pepper, pink peppercorns and yoghurt and chill until nearly set. Then spread the mixture over the salmon and roll up tightly in the paper, twist the ends around like a cracker and fold the ends neatly underneath.

Chill until needed.

Carefully unwrap the roulade and slice up onto six pretty plates. I think two slices each looks nice or three very little ones is fun too. Decorate with little flowers made from tomato skin peelings and tiny sprigs of parsley.

Roast Mallard with Cinnamon and Cloves

Serves 6

This recipe is suitable for any kind of duck or duck portions if you are in a hurry.

Set oven at 200 C, 400 F, Gas Mark 6

> 3 mallard, prepared
> Olive oil
> 1 small onion, finely chopped
> 3 heaped tablespoons runny honey
> 1 full glass white wine
> Salt and pepper
> 2 teaspoons ground cloves
> 2 teaspoon ground cinnamon

Place the mallard in the oil in a roasting tin with the onion. Rub each bird with oil, cloves and cinnamon and then spoon over the honey and season with salt and pepper. Pour the wine into the pan with another glass full of water and roast in the oven for 40 minutes until the skins are crispy but the birds are just pink inside. Remove the birds from the roasting tin and carve. Arrange the meat in an attractive fan shape on each plate with a crispy leg each and keep warm while you boil up the juices, scraping the pan on the hob. Pour off any excess fat before correcting the seasoning and spooning the sauce over the duck. Serve immediately. You can top up the sauce with more wine if required.

Creamed Potatoes
Serves 8

Just a touch more up-market than mashed potatoes, a little indulgence that is always appreciated.

> 1.5 kg old potatoes, peeled
> Salt, pepper and nutmeg to taste
> 150 ml milk
> 150 ml cream
> 75 g butter

Cook the potatoes in salted boiling water until soft. Drain, return to pan and mash with all the remaining ingredients until smooth. I usually use an electric whisk at this stage to make it really creamy.

Baby Sweetcorn and Parisienne Carrots in Chive Butter
Serves 8

> 450 g baby or Parisienne carrots
> 3 x 125 g packets baby sweetcorn
> 50 g butter
> 1 bunch chives
> Juice of $^1/_2$ orange
> Salt and pepper

Peel and trim the carrots. Trim the sweetcorn to matching lengths. Boil the vegetables separately in salted water until al dente. Chop the chives into a bowl, add the orange juice, salt and pepper. Drain the vegetables and mix together in a warm dish with the butter and spoon over the chives and juice. Cover with clingfilm and keep warm.

Valentine Hearts with Blackcurrant Coulis

Serves 10

Use heart-shaped tin moulds and choose plates that are large enough to turn the moulds onto with room to spoon the sauce around.

> 10 heart-shaped tin moulds
> 2 x 450 g Greek strained yoghurt
> Grated rind of ¹/₂ a lemon
> Few drops vanilla essence
> 3 level tablespoons of clear honey
> 11 g sachet gelatine
> 150 ml double cream, whipped
>
> *Blackcurrant Coulis*
> 454 g frozen blackcurrants
> 125 g sugar
> Kirsch

Line each mould with greaseproof paper or clingfilm. Dissolve the gelatine according to instructions. Then fold the remaining ingredients together and stir in the gelatine. Spoon the mixture into each mould and chill to set.

Turn the hearts out onto plates and spoon around the coulis. To make the coulis, briefly cook the blackcurrants with sugar. Cool and liquidize. Sieve the sauce and add a dash of kirsch, cover and keep chilled until needed.

ROMANTIC ANNIVERSARY DINNER FOR TWO OR FOUR

Now's the time to make up for any lack of attention to the other half! Spoil him with a wonderful candlelit dinner, wear his favourite scent and your best dress.

If you are the husband preparing this delightful evening, then wear some thing she gave you and bring her some lovely red roses which she can sigh over. You can't fail!

MENU

*   Scallops in basil sauce

*   Duck breasts with lemon and limes
       New potatoes
       Mangetouts or sugar snap peas

       Grand Marnier and passion fruit soufflé

This menu is perfect for last minute cooking. When you have made your dining room look lovely for this special occasion you can start preparing the food. Make the soufflé mix up to the stage indicated in the recipe and have

A Romantic Dinner a Deux

everything ready for last minute activity. Then start to cook the potatoes followed by the duck breasts and lastly the vegetables. Keep everything warm and finally just before sitting down cook the scallops together over a glass of bubbly or wine.

Wine: *Loire, 1989 Muscadet Sur Lie, Jacques Guindon*
         Beaujolais, 1988 Saint Amour, Thorin
         Australia, 1989 Brown Bros. Orange Muscat & Flora

Scallops in Basil Sauce
Serves 4

For added chic, serve the scallops in scrubbed shells, or pretty white shells, available from most good hardware stores.

          3 jumbo scallops each
          Salt and freshly ground black pepper
          150 ml Muscadet
          50 g fresh basil leaves, shredded
          50 g butter, in pieces

Poach the scallops in the wine, with half the basil and the seasoning, for three minutes. Carefully lift them out and keep warm whilst you reduce the liquor to half its volume. Add the remaining basil leaves. Bring the sauce to the boil, then reduce the heat to very low and whisk in the butter until it has melted and thickened the sauce. Adjust the seasoning and let the scallops sit in the sauce for a minute and then spoon into the shells and serve immediately.

Duck Breasts with Lemon and Limes

Serves 4

I prefer to use duck breasts because there is no wastage and less fat and they are much easier to cook than a whole duck.

> 2 duck breast fillets
> Salt and pepper
> Olive oil
> 1 clove garlic, crushed
> 350 g fresh spinach, washed and dried
> Nutmeg
> 25 g butter
> 1 wine glass Noilly Prat Vermouth
> 150 ml lime cordial
> 2 lemons, rind and juice
> 2 limes coarsely grated
> A little stock or water

Season the duck breasts with salt and pepper. Sauté in a big frying pan in two tablespoons of olive oil with the garlic. Cook until tender. Cook the spinach, drain and season with salt, pepper and nutmeg. Add the butter and keep warm. Drain off any excess oil from the pan and stir in the vermouth and lime cordial. Squeeze the lemons and add the juice to the pan, with the grated lemon and lime. Simmer for a couple of minutes. Peel the limes and cut into segments and stir into the sauce. Add a little stock or water to increase the volume of sauce. Simmer until the sauce has thickened, carve the duck breasts and arrange the slices on a small bed of spinach on individual plates with the lime sauce poured over.

Grand Marnier and Passion Fruit Soufflé

Serves 4

This is a truly exceptional soufflé and worth all the bother. In fact, soufflés are very easy, practice makes perfect!

Set oven at 200 C, 400 F, Gas Mark 6

> 50 g butter
> 50 g flour
> 300 ml milk
> 50 g sugar
> 5 eggs, separated
> 1 extra egg white
> 5 tablespoons Grand Marnier
> 8 passion fruit
> Icing sugar
> Extra butter
> Pinch of salt

Brush the inside of the soufflé dish with the extra butter and tie a collar of greaseproof paper around the dish and secure tightly. Melt the butter in a saucepan over a high heat, stir in the flour and gradually beat in the milk. Remove from the heat and stir until smooth. Beat in the sugar and egg yolks until smooth, then add the Grand Marnier. Cut the passion fruit in half and squeeze all the juice and pips into the mixture. Whisk all the egg whites until stiff with a pinch of salt and gently fold into the mixture. Spoon this into the soufflé dish and bake on a tray for 25 minutes or until well risen, just set and browned. Quickly remove the paper, dust lightly with icing sugar, and serve immediately.

SHROVE TUESDAY PANCAKE PARTY FOR EIGHT

Pancakes are fun. You can make them the day before, cover and chill them until needed. Separate each one with a layer of greaseproof paper to prevent them sticking to each other. Then you can fill the savoury pancakes in the evening and set aside ready to heat through in the oven. Much more fun of course is to make the mixture in advance and to let everybody make and toss their own leaving them to fill the crêpes themselves. Have the filling and the sauce ready for your guests to dip into.

MENU

*   Roquefort and pecan salad

       Veal and olive casserole

*   Wild rice
*   Aromatic carrots with cloves

       Apricot crêpes with walnut marmalade sauce

As it is such an informal evening you can do this all at the last minute if you want to. Although I always like to do the shopping the day before and I would make the casserole too. However, the quickest way to do it is to make the casserole first and prepare the vegetables while this is cooking. Make the pancake batter, warm through the jam and leave it in the saucepan and make the sauce and leave it ready to heat through. Lastly make up the salads and put them on the table ready for your guests.

Wine: *Italy, 1985 Villa Antinori, Chianti Classico Riserva*
               Rhône, 1988 Muscat de Beaumes de Venise, Domaine
                  de Coyeux

Roquefort and Pecan Salad

Serves 6-8

All sorts of new varieties of lettuces keep rearing their heads and I do try to keep up with the latest ingredients. It is such fun to have all sorts of shapes, flavours and textures mixed into a salad.

> 350 g Roquefort, trimmed
> 125 g Pecans
> 1 whole Batavia lettuce, washed
> 1 whole Lollo Rosso lettuce, washed
> A good handful of Lambs lettuce, washed
> Walnut oil vinaigrette, (page 81)
> A little chopped parsley
> Walnut oil

Trim the lettuce leaves and arrange in attractive shapes on six plates. Sauté the pecans in a tablespoon of walnut oil to brown them. Drain on absorbent paper and sprinkle them onto the salads. Chop up the Roquefort and dot all over the salads. Spoon over the vinaigrette and parsley and serve with fresh bread and unsalted butter.

Veal and Olive Casserole

Serves 8

Stewing veal is very reasonably priced and makes delicious pies and casseroles.

905 g packet Bonduelle frozen baby onions
2 tablespoons olive oil
1 clove crushed garlic
Salt and pepper
Oregano and 1 bay-leaf
900 g pie veal in cubes
1 heaped tablespoon flour
300 ml red wine
300 ml chicken stock
Few drops of chilli sauce
2 heaped tablespoons tomato purée
3 orange peppers, trimmed and sliced
400 g stuffed olives
2 tablespoons chopped parsley

In a large casserole or saucepan cook the onions in the oil until soft. Add the garlic, seasoning and herbs. Add the veal and brown all over. Stir in the flour and then the wine, stock, chilli, tomato purée and peppers. Cook for about an hour and when the veal is tender add the olives. Simmer for a couple of minutes, sprinkle with parsley and serve with fresh buttered pasta, rice or potatoes.

Wild Rice

Serves 8

A small amount of wild rice adds a lot of style to plain rice which can be rather boring on its own.

> 225 g American Easy Cook rice
> 50 g River Brand Wild Rice
> 1 chicken stock cube
> 50 g butter
> Black pepper
> 1 tablespoon chopped parsley

Cook the rice and the wild rice together in enough boiling water with the stock cube for 12 minutes. Drain and refresh with just a little hot water. Transfer to a warm serving dish and mix in the butter and pepper and sprinkle with the parsley. Cover with clingfilm to keep warm until needed.

Aromatic Carrots with Cloves

Serves 8

Lucy James produced this recipe at a dinner party and I was so impressed by the subtle flavours that I have had to copy her idea!

The smaller the sticks of carrot the more professional it looks. It is worth another ten minutes for a dinner party.

900 g English carrots
1 tablespoon chopped parsley
Black pepper

Have the following ingredients in a saucer ready to add to the carrots
1 teaspoon grated lemon rind
Juice of 1 lemon
2 teaspoons sugar
1 teaspoon whole cloves
Pinch of salt
1 tablespoon butter

Top, tail and peel the carrots and cut into half and then into sticks. Boil in salted water and drain, immediately tip back into the pan and add all the ingredients on the saucer. Seal with the lid and leave for ten minutes for the steam to release the flavours of the cloves into the carrots. Briefly reheat on a high temperature, shaking the pan so the carrots don't stick to the bottom and transfer them to a warm dish and serve sprinkled with chopped parsley and black pepper.

Apricot Crêpes with Walnut Marmalade Sauce
Serves 8

454 g apricot preserve
Juice of 1 lemon
454 g orange marmalade
Juice of 1 large orange
100 g walnut pieces
3 tablespoons Cointreau
Butter, caster sugar and oil if needed

Pancakes
225 g plain flour, sieved
Pinch of salt
2 eggs
600 ml milk
1 tablespoon vegetable oil

First make the filling; melt the apricot preserve with the lemon juice. Now make the sauce. Melt the marmalade slowly with the orange, juice and walnuts in another pan. Bring to the boil for a few minutes and add the Cointreau. Remove from heat and leave to cool. Make the pancake batter by mixing the flour, salt, eggs and oil together in a big bowl and gradually stirring in the milk. Leave for ten minutes or more to settle. Sieve the mixture to remove any lumps and transfer the batter to a good pouring jug. Heat a few drops of oil in a large non-stick frying pan and make eight to ten big pancakes. As each one is ready, fill with the apricot mixture. Fold in half and half again and pour over the marmalade sauce. Serve the pancakes as soon as they are all ready.

Alternatively, make the pancakes well in advance and arrange in a buttered ovenproof dish.

Just before serving them, dot with butter and sprinkle with caster sugar and place in a hot oven to reheat. Serve the sauce separately.

A FISHY EVENING

There are to be found on some market stalls the most fascinating varieties of tropical and game fish. Fierce and spiky or bright blue and stripy, they come from all over the world for us to try. The trouble is most people take one look at them and presume that it is too difficult to cook and so buy a slab of cod instead. Which is a great pity because the textures and flavours of these fish are quite different. So be brave, next time you see a funny fish, ask what it is and how to cook it, bring it home to try, you can always BBQ or grill it with dried herbs, lemon juice and olive oil. Just turn it over once and when both sides are crispy and the flesh comes away easily from the bones, the fish is ready to eat. Serve with a good salad or crunchy vegetables.

The most important thing is to check that your choice of fish is really fresh. Preferably brought in that morning, because then you get the true flavour and the fish literally melts in your mouth. Only, however if you don't overcook it which most people tend to do. Fish and seafood is so delicate, it must be either steamed or poached very gently so that it is full of moisture and flavour or grilled/fried very quickly to seal in the juices and prevent it from drying out and becoming tasteless. Here are a few exciting ways of trying these fish.

SUMMER MENU FOR SIX

* Mock Mediterranean fish soup
   Grilled Red Snapper with sweet red onions
* Warm green beans and mustard seed vinaigrette
   New potatoes
   Redcurrant and whitecurrant sorbet

Wine: *Italy 1989 Soave Classico, Guerrieri-Rizzardi*
    New Zealand, 1989 Ngatarawa Sauvignon
    Loire, 1986 Vouvray, Domaine Allias, Moelleux

WINTER MENU FOR SIX

Prawns, spring onion and ginger in filo pastry
John Dory with sweet pepper sauce
*   Warm green beans with mustard seed vinaigrette
New potatoes
Individual chocolate pecan pies and crème chantilly

Wine: *Sherry, Manzanilla de Sanlúcar*
White Rioja, 1985 Blanco Seco, CVNE
Eau de Vie, Mirabell, Alfred Schladerer

Make either pudding the day before, so you have time to go to a market to choose the fresh fish on the day of the party. Keep it cool until needed otherwise it will get a distinctly fishy smell which, I can assure you from past experience, will linger for ages.

Prepare your vegetables first then make the starter and lastly the main course. Start with the pepper sauce then cook the fish and the vegetables. These menus are ideal for informal evenings only.

A Fishy Evening

Mock Mediterranean Fish Soup
Serves 8

Unlike most fish soups this is very quick and easy to cook but, of course, this does tend to mean that it is a little more expensive.

450 g Monkfish fillets
450 g fresh scallops
100 g butter
Salt and pepper
Branch of fresh thyme
Handful of fresh dill
1 bayleaf
A little sprinkle of cayenne pepper
3 tablespoons tomato purée
2 x 397 g tins chopped tomatoes
600 ml water
1 dessertspoon caster sugar

Trim the Monkfish of any skin or membrane, cut into four strips and slice into small pieces. Clean the scallops and chop into similar sized pieces.

Melt the butter and add all the seasoning and herbs according to how highly flavoured you like your food. Add the fish and sauté for one to two minutes. Add the chopped tomatoes and gently blend together. Stir in the tomato purée and 600 ml of water and lastly the caster sugar. Bring the soup to the boil but then reduce to a simmer for about 20 minutes. Add a little more water and remove the bayleaf. Serve with hot, crusty garlic or herb bread.

Grilled Red Snapper with Sweet Red Onions

Serves 6

3 x 900 g Red Snapper, gutted and washed
Olive oil
4 medium red onions, peeled
2 medium red peppers, ends and seeds removed
3 tablespoons olive oil
1 clove garlic, crushed
Fresh thyme
Salt and pepper
3 tablespoons Balsamic vinegar of Modena

Remove the head of the fish at a neat angle and trim the flaps of skin. Rinse the fish in cold water and pat dry with kitchen paper. Lay them on an oiled baking tray. Now sprinkle the fish with oil, salt, pepper and thyme. Grill under medium heat until cooked through, about ten minutes. Now turn the fish over and repeat the same process.

Meanwhile finely slice the onions and the peppers and cook together until soft and slightly browned in a large frying pan with three tablespoons of oil. Now add a little crushed garlic, salt and pepper and cook for a further minute and lastly add the Balsamic vinegar. Fry for one minute, add three tablespoons of water and remove from the heat. Remove the tail and fins from the fish and cut each side of the fish in half across so you have four nice diamond shaped portions to each fish. Carefully lift the flesh from the bones and set the fillets of snapper on to warm plates. Quickly sauté the onions again and then spoon them to one side of the red snapper and serve immediately.

Warm Green Beans and Mustard Seed Vinaigrette
Serves 6

This is delicious served warm as a side salad for a fish dish or with grilled meat and equally good as a chilled salad on its own.

500 g Kenyan fine beans
Salt and pepper
1 tablespoon mustard seeds
2-3 tablespoons walnut oil

Top and tail the beans and cook in salted boiling water until al dente. Drain, put into a warm dish and spoon over the oil, pepper and mustard seeds. Cover with clingfilm to keep warm.

Redcurrant and Whitecurrant Sorbet
Serves 8

450 g redcurrants
375 g whitecurrants
225 g caster sugar
300 ml cheapest Ruby Port
300 ml water
2 large slices of lemon peel
1 egg white, stiffly beaten
Fresh fruit and fresh mint to decorate
1 box Tuiles d'Amandes, to serve

Remove the stalks and put the currants into a saucepan. Add the sugar, Port, water and lemon peel. Bring to the boil for 15 minutes. Leave the currants to cool. Remove the lemon peel and purée the currants in the Magimix and then sieve, to make sure that there are no pips or stalks and return it to the deep freeze. When the sorbet is nearly frozen fold in the beaten egg white and transfer the sorbet into a container and seal until needed.

Serve scoops of the sorbet on each plate decorated with fresh fruit and mint and hand around the Tuiles d'Amandes separately.

Prawns, Spring Onions and Ginger
in Filo Pastry
Serves 6

An unusual starter with an oriental flavour, particularly good before lamb dishes.

Set oven at 200 C, 400 F, Gas Mark 6

> 1 bunch spring onions, washed and trimmed
> 454 g large frozen prawns, thawed
> 8 sheets filo pastry
> Olive oil
> 100 g butter
> Plenty of grated ginger
> Plenty of crushed garlic
> Salt, pepper and cayenne pepper
> 1 lemon and a few spring onions for decoration

Slice the spring onions thinly and drain the prawns. Place half of the pastry on an oiled non-stick baking tray. Brush the pastry with plenty of oil. Sprinkle the onions along the centre of the pastry.

In a saucepan melt the butter and add the ginger, garlic, salt and pepper and cook for a couple of minutes. Heap the prawns over the onions. Pour the butter over the prawns, cover with the remaining pastry, brush with more oil and roll up the pastry. Tucking in the ends. Sprinkle with cayenne pepper and bake in the oven until the pastry is brown and crispy. Serve immediately on a plate decorated with very finely sliced lemon and wisps of spring onion.

John Dory with Sweet Pepper Sauce

Serves 6

Apart from being one of the most unattractive fish I have come across the John Dory is one of the most delicious! Ask your fishmonger to cut off the head and clean the fish for you.

Set oven at 200 C, 400 F, Gas Mark 6

> 3 John Dory (about 2 kg in total)
> Lemon juice, salt and pepper and butter
> Watercress and lemon to decorate
>
> *Sweet Pepper Sauce*
> 2 tablespoons oil
> 1 onion, finely chopped
> 750 g ripe tomatoes, skinned
> 2 teaspoons caster sugar
> Salt and pepper
> 250 g red peppers, seeds removed and chopped
> 500 ml boiling water

Gently cook the onions until soft in the oil. Chop up the tomatoes and add them to the onions with the sugar, salt and pepper. Simmer for ten minutes, add the peppers and simmer with the water for 20 minutes.

Rinse the fish under cold water and bake wrapped in foil with lemon juice, salt, pepper and butter for 15 minutes. Remove from the oven and cool slightly before lifting fish on to a flat dish or board to remove the skin. Carefully lift off the fish fillets from the bones and arrange neatly on six warm plates.

Liquidize the sauce and heat through before spooning around the fish. Decorate with watercress and lemon.

Individual Chocolate Pecan Pies and Crème Chantilly
Serves 10

Set oven at 190 C, 375 F, Gas Mark 5

454 g packet Saxby's fresh shortcrust pastry
10 x 6 cm baking tins greased and lined with Bakewell paper

Filling

75 g plain chocolate	$1/4$ teaspoon salt
3 eggs	75 g butter
225 g soft dark brown sugar	6 tablespoons golden syrup
1 teaspoon vanilla extract	200 g shelled pecan nuts, coarsely chopped

Melt the chocolate over very low heat. Roll out the pastry on a floured board and line the tins with the pastry and trim. Prick tiny holes in the base. In a large bowl beat the eggs, then add the sugar, vanilla and salt. Melt the butter with the chocolate, add the syrup and chopped nuts, mix well and add to the eggs and sugar. Beat together and pour the mixture into the pastry cases and bake for 30 minutes or until the filling is set. Leave the pies to cool and chill if necessary to help you to lift them out of their tins. Place the pies on a flat baking tray to warm them through at the last minute. Serve with the crème chantilly.

Crème Chantilly
Serves 10

600 ml double cream
1 teaspoon vanilla essence
2 or 3 tablespoons sifted icing sugar

Whip the double cream until it forms soft peaks and fold in the vanilla essence and icing sugar. Spoon into a pretty bowl and decorate with rose petals for special occasions.

SURPRISE BIRTHDAY PARTY FOR EIGHT

I love giving my friends surprise birthday parties as much as I like being given them myself. You can have great fun tying helium balloons on the back of each chair or in a huge knot in the centre of the table instead of flowers and much more fun. Silly little presents, party poppers and games add to the frivolity but good food and wine is the ultimate compliment. Here are a couple of menus for you to try. You can make the desserts the day before then stick some candles in at the last minute.

WINTER MENU

Pheasant mousselines in Cumberland sauce
Fillet of beef, tomatoes and courgettes en croûte
Frozen or fresh croquette potatoes
Frozen spinach
*   Chocolate biscuit cake

Wine: *Red Burgundy, 1986 Hautes Côtes de Nuits, Les Vignes Hautes, Moillard*
Red Burgundy, 1983 Chambolle-Musigny, Doudet-Naudin
Calvados, Busnel Vieille Réserve

SUMMER MENU

*   Grilled goat's cheese and rosemary salad
Salmon en croûte with dill Hollandaise sauce
Mangetouts
New potatoes
Tayberry and almond roulade

Wine: *Beaujolais, 1989 Fleurie, Thorin*
Red Loire, 1986 Bourgueil, Domaine du Grand Clos, Audebert et Fils
Jurançon, 1982 Prestige d'Automne, Vendange Tardive

Pheasant Mousselines with Cumberland Sauce

Serves 8

This is an excellent way of using up old pheasants from the deep freeze.

Set oven at 190 C, 375 F, Gas Mark 5

> 250 g pheasant meat
> Salt, pepper and nutmeg
> 1 whole egg
> 2 egg whites
> 284 ml double cream
> Butter
> Bakewell paper

> *Cumberland Sauce*
> Rind and juice of 2 oranges
> Rind and juice of 1 lemon
> 340 g redcurrant jelly
> 1 large glass of Port
> 2 tablespoons of cornflour
> 2 tablespoons Grand Marnier

Make the mousselines first. Purée the meat in the Magimix until very smooth and season. Add the whole egg and the egg whites. Blend for a minute and chill the mixture in the bowl of the Magimix for 15 minutes. Briefly blend the cream into the pheasant and chill for a further 15 minutes. Grease eight ramekins with butter and line with circles of Bakewell paper. Fill each ramekin with the pheasant mixture and bake in a bain-marie for 25 minutes or until set.

Use less redcurrant jelly in the sauce if you do not have a sweet tooth.

Pare the orange and lemon rinds into very thin strips and blanch for five minutes in boiling water. Strain and refresh under cold water. Put the redcurrant jelly into the pan with the fruit juice and bring to the boil. Simmer for four minutes, add the Port and stir in the cornflour mixed with three tablespoons of water. Add the blanched rind and simmer for five minutes. Stir in the Grand Marnier and remove from the heat. Turn the moulds on to warm plates, pour the sauce over each mousseline and serve immediately.

Fillet of Beef, Tomatoes and Courgettes en Croûte

Serves 6-8

This recipe makes a delicious change from Beef Wellington, the unusual combination catches everyone's attention which is always nice for the cook!

Set oven at 200 C, 400 F, Gas Mark 6

950 g fillet beef	*Watercress sauce*
2 tablespoons olive oil	$^1/_2$ very small onion, finely chopped
397 g tin chopped tomatoes	2 bunches watercress, trimmed and washed
350 g courgettes, grated	50 g butter
$^1/_2$ small onion, finely chopped	25 g flour
15 g fresh basil, chopped	450 ml double cream
1 clove garlic, crushed	1 wine glass Noilly Prat vermouth
Salt and pepper	Salt, pepper and nutmeg
2 tablespoons brandy	$^1/_2$ teaspoon sugar
500 g packet fresh puff pastry	Juice of $^1/_2$ lemon
1 egg, beaten	Extra milk

Trim the fillet of beef. Quickly sauté the meat in the oil on all sides, remove from the pan and leave to cool. In the pan slowly cook the onion, courgettes, tomatoes, garlic and basil and simmer for five minutes. Season and stir in the brandy. Cook for ten minutes.

Roll out the pastry and place in the centre of a non-stick baking tray or tin. Spoon the tomato mixture on to the middle of the pastry leaving enough to cover the beef fillet. Place the beef on top of the tomato mixture and spread with the rest. Fold the pastry over the meat, brush with beaten egg and bake for 35 minutes or until the pastry is golden and crisp and the beef rare.

Meanwhile, make the sauce. Cook the onions in the butter until soft but do not brown. Stir in the watercress and then the flour, gradually stir in the vermouth and the cream until you have a smooth sauce. Cook over low heat for five minutes. Cool slightly and liquidize with a little extra milk to thin the sauce if necessary. Season to taste, add the sugar and lemon juice. Serve the sauce separately with the fillet of beef.

Chocolate Biscuit Cake

Serves 8 - 12

This is really playschool stuff, an ideal recipe for bored children in the school holidays to try. However it's always advisable to negotiate terms over the washing up!

350 g plain chocolate
3 tablespoons golden syrup
350 g butter
3 tablespoons cocoa powder
350 g digestive biscuits, broken up
50 g seedless raisins
50 g mixed peel
100 g glacé cherries, halved
100 g hazelnut kernels, halved
extra hazelnuts or glacé cherries
300 ml whipped cream
Angelica to decorate
Oil

First oil and line a large terrine or cake tin with Bakewell paper, failing that line a 2 kg sized Flora margarine tub with clingfilm and pour the mixture into it.

Break up the chocolate and melt very slowly in a non-stick saucepan. Add the syrup, butter and cocoa. Mix together and cool slightly. Mix in the biscuits, fruits, and hazelnuts. Turn the mixture into the tin and refrigerate until firm.

Turn out the cake, smooth it all over using a hot palette knife. Decorate with piped rosettes of cream, toasted hazelnuts or glacé cherries and angelica to suit occasion.

Grilled Goat's Cheese and Rosemary Salad
Serves 8

Make sure the cheese is not too ripe and smelly and refrigerate it until needed so that it is easier to handle.

> 4 x 60 g Crottins de Chavignol goat's cheese
> 8 slices of brown bread
> Fresh rosemary
> 3 x 100 g packets Sainsbury's frisée and radicchio salad mix
> 1 packet edible fresh nasturtium blooms or lamb's lettuce
> Walnut oil vinaigrette (page 81)

Arrange all the salad mixtures together on eight plates and sprinkle with walnut oil vinaigrette. Cut each goat's cheese into two thick rounds and place a leaf or two of rosemary on each one. Trim the crusts from the bread and cut into a suitable size in proportion to the plate of salad. Grill the toast on one side and then place the cheese on the untoasted side and grill for five minutes until slightly bubbling. Carefully place each piece of toast on to the salad and serve immediately.

Salmon en Croûte with Dill Hollandaise Sauce

Serves 10

Set oven at 190 C, 375 F, Gas Mark 5

Large bunch fresh dill weed, chopped
2.5 kg salmon to be filleted and skinned
2 x 454 g packets puff pastry
1 beaten egg
100 g butter
Flour

Hollandaise Sauce
3 egg yolks
Black pepper and salt
1 lemon, squeezed
225 g unsalted butter, melted

Lay out your cleaned salmon fillets and pick out any bones you can find, tweezers or fingers are fine. Season each fillet with salt and pepper and a third of the dill. Roll out the pastry on a floured surface into two large rectangles about two and a half centimetres bigger all round than the fish. Place one piece of pastry on a greased floured baking tray and lay a fillet squarely on it. Dot the salmon with half the butter and cover with the other salmon laying it in the opposite direction and folding the end under to make a neat parcel. Dot with the remaining butter and another one third dill. Cover with the pastry and seal it with the beaten egg and glaze all over. Make any decorations you like and a little hole for the steam to escape at the top. Bake for about 35 minutes until the pastry is golden. Leave the fish to settle and cool down for ten minutes before serving. During this time you can make the Hollandaise sauce.

Hollandaise Sauce
Put the egg yolks, seasoning, lemon juice and remaining dill into a food processor and blend. Bring the butter to boiling point and pour gradually into the eggs, beating all the time until the sauce is thick and glossy. Leave for a couple of minutes. Give it a quick whiz and serve in a sauce boat.

Tayberry and Almond Roulade

Serves 6-8

I love this pudding and I make it for most of the dinner parties that I cater for because it is so light and I always decorate it with a single red rose.

Set oven at 190 C, 375 F, Gas Mark 5

> 4 eggs, separated
> 125 g caster sugar
> 125 g ground almonds
> 1 teaspoon baking powder
> 1 tablespoon Langdale's Essence of Rosewater
> Few drops almond essence
> 125 g fresh tayberries
> 300 ml double cream, whipped
> Icing sugar, sieved
> Extra whipping cream to decorate
>
> *Tayberry Sauce*
> 225 g tayberries
> 2 tablespoons Cointreau
> 1 tablespoon caster sugar

Line a Swiss roll tin with Bakewell paper and secure. Whisk the egg whites, add half the sugar slowly and whisk until stiff. Beat the egg yolks with the remaining sugar until white and fluffy, add the essences. Fold in the ground almonds and baking powder and then fold in the egg whites and spread evenly. Bake for 20 minutes until firm to touch. Allow to cool slightly before turning on to a large sugared sheet of Bakewell paper. Roll up and secure until cool.

Carefully remove the paper and trim the edges. Spread the inside with cream and tayberries and roll up again and place on a serving dish to decorate with rosettes of whipped cream and six to eight tayberries reserved from the sauce ingredients.

Chill until needed.

Now make the sauce. Liquidize the tayberries with the Cointreau and sugar with two tablespoons of water. Sieve the sauce to remove the pips. Serve the sauce in a sauceboat with the chilled roulade.

SIMPLE SEDUCTION CUISINE
FOR TWO

The food and setting of this subtle seduction must be carefully planned to achieve the best results! Avoid heavy, fatty, spicy, coarse, indigestible foods and instead play on soft fresh ingredients (lightly cooked or raw) like scallops, asparagus, oysters and soft fruit. Avoid complicated menus so that you are fresh and relaxed for your companion and most of all, get into the romantic mood with a soft warm and cosy atmosphere. The food can look after itself.

MENU

*   Pâté de foie aux truffes salade with pink peppercorn vinaigrette
*   Lobster in saffron cream sauce
        A side dish of fresh asparagus and butter

Fresh raspberries or strawberries and cream
or
Bunches of fresh grapes and peaches

Wine: *Champagne to start with - the best you can afford - which you can drink beforehand, with the pâté de foie salade and - with a bit of luck - after the dinner as well.*
Then, a really good white Burgundy, like 1985 Puligny-Montrachet, Les Folatières, Prosper Maufoux.
Finally a half bottle of deliciously extravagent Sauternes - 1985 Ch. Lafaurie-Peyraguey if your budget doesn't stretch to Ch. d'Yquem.
Expensive, but think how much you have saved by not going to a restaurant!

When you have laid the table and got the drinks and wines ready, then you can start by arranging the soft fruit on some pretty glass or china and whip up some cream. Get your coffee tray all sorted out and then prepare the starter and place on the table.

Now cook the asparagus and drench in butter and simply cover in clingfilm to keep warm. Lastly tackle the lobster. This can sit for a bit in the frying pan until you are ready to heat it through and serve.

Pâté de foie aux Truffes Salade with Pink Peppercorn Vinaigrette

Serves 4

As this recipe involves no cooking whatsoever it is ideal for hectic hosts or hostesses wishing to produce something glamorous but easy.

A selection of
Lambs lettuce, washed and trimmed
Oak leaf lettuce, washed and trimmed
Frisée lettuce, washed and trimmed
$^1/_2$ packet of Phileas Fogg Mignon Morçeaux
228 g tin Le Parfait pâté with truffles
Walnut oil vinaigrette (page 81)
4 teaspoons pink peppercorns

Arrange the salads attractively on each plate. Slice the pâté into 12 thin pieces and place them in the centre of the salad, overlapping each other. Add the mignons morçeaux to the lettuce leaves and sprinkle with the vinaigrette, carefully spooning the pink peppercorns on to the slices of pâté. This also makes a nice summer main course for two people.

Lobster in Saffron Cream Sauce

Serves 2

The ultimate in seafood, the lobster deserves to be eaten in the simplest way possible.

2 cooked and prepared lobsters
2 shallots, peeled and finely chopped
50 g butter
A good pinch of saffron
Salt and pepper
150 ml medium dry white wine
Juice of $1/2$ a lemon
150 ml double cream
Extra butter
Cayenne pepper

Cook the shallots gently in butter with saffron until soft, add the salt and pepper, wine and lemon juice. Meanwhile pull out the lobster meat and cut into manageable pieces and stir into the mixture. As this reheats you can stir in the cream and increase the temperature slightly and bubble for a few minutes.

Spoon this back into the lobster shells and dot with a little extra butter and sprinkle with cayenne pepper.

Place the lobsters and claws under the grill. By the time the lobsters are brown and crispy on top the claws will have warmed through. Serve immediately.

NEARLY EASTER DINNER PARTY FOR TWELVE

A time for chocolate indulgences, daffodils and spring lamb so incorporate all these things in your menus. You can arrange branches of blossoms along the table with little gold Easter eggs nestling in them. You can also buy small mock birds nests or twig wreaths which you can place in front of each guest filled with tiny speckled coloured chocolate eggs. Cook the best Welsh or English lamb as it is far superior to anything else.

MENU

Chilled almond and chive soup
* Rack of lamb in ginger, honey and herb glaze
* Carrot and cumin purée
* Creamed potatoes (page 42)
White chocolate ice cream with cookies

Wine: *Sherry, Fino*
            Red Bordeaux, 1985 Ch. Rouet
            Eau de Vie, Williams Birne, Alfred Schladerer

Make the soup a day in advance so that it is really chilled. Double up the main course recipe and vegetables but the ice cream will feed everybody. If you haven't got any help for this party a lot of organisation and advance planning is needed. Make the ice cream a few days in advance and the cookies the night before and keep in an airtight container. You can make the purées the night before and reheat them from room temperature half an hour before dinner while the lamb is cooking. Last of all put the bowls of soup on the table so you can join your guests when they arrive and sit down as soon as you are ready.

Chilled Almond and Chive Soup

You will probably think this is the most extraordinary combination of ingredients but I do assure you that everybody who has tried it has loved it.

150 g flaked almonds
600 ml milk
1 clove garlic, crushed
1 large onion, finely sliced
100 g butter
2 tablespoons plain flour
1 litre chicken stock
Salt and pepper
600 ml double cream
3 tablespoons chopped chives
Extra cream and snipped chives for decoration

Finely chop the almonds, scald the milk, add the garlic and nuts, cover the pan and leave to infuse. Slowly cook the onions in the butter until soft. Mix in the flour and gradually beat in the stock. Stir until boiling and season. Liquidize the stock and then liquidize the milk, garlic and nuts and whisk into the stock. Return to the saucepan, stir in cream and chives and reheat slowly so the flavours develop. Simmer for 20 minutes and then remove from the heat and leave to cool. Adjust seasoning then chill the soup until needed. Serve with swirls of extra cream and a few snipped chives.

Rack of Lamb in Ginger, Honey and Herb Glaze

Serves 6

Ginger, as you may gather through this book, is one of my favourite spices. I use it as much as possible in both my sweet and savoury recipes.

Set oven at 190 C, 375 F, Gas Mark 5

2 or 3 racks of lamb, 6 bones in each
3 tablespoons olive oil
1 medium root ginger, peeled and grated
Grated rind of 1 lemon
Juice of 2 lemons
4 tablespoons runny honey
Salt and pepper
Fresh thyme
1 glass dry white wine
1 glass water

Smear the rack of lamb with the olive oil, ginger and lemon rind and place in a roasting dish. Pour over the rest of the oil and season with salt and pepper and fresh thyme. Add one glass white wine and one glass water to the pan and roast in the oven for 15 minutes. Now trickle the honey over the lamb and top up the pan juices with the lemon juice. Return to the oven for a further 15 minutes. The skin should be crispy and the lamb pink with just enough juices to serve spooned over the meat.

Carve the lamb into three chops each and arrange on warm plates with a few spoonfuls of the glaze and decorate accordingly.

Carrot and Cumin Purée

Serves 6

This recipe doubles up nicely for a dinner party of twelve and I also like to use it to accompany the Sunday lunch roast.

> 1.1 kg English carrots
> Salt and pepper
> 1 1/2 teaspoons Rajah ground cumin
> 50 g butter
> 50 ml double cream
> A little chopped parsley

Peel and chop the carrots, boil in salted water until soft. Drain, cool fractionally, put into the food processor and blend until puréed. Season with salt, pepper and cumin. Blend in butter and cream and transfer to warm serving dish. Seal with clingfilm to keep warm. Sprinkle with chopped parsley before serving.

White Chocolate Ice Cream with Cookies
Serves 12

This ice cream is like eating white velvet, quite dreamy, so do try it. It is also excellent with Marks and Spencer's chocolate sauce, heated up, which is available in 500 g cartons.

Set oven at 200 C, 400 F, Gas Mark 6

300 g bar white chocolate
4 large egg yolks
175 g caster sugar
568 ml double cream
10 tablespoons milk
A few drops vanilla essence
284 ml whipped cream

White chocolate cookies
75 g unsalted butter
75 g light brown sugar
75 g caster sugar
1 egg
1 teaspoon vanilla essence
175 g plain flour
$^1/_2$ teaspoon baking powder
$^1/_4$ teaspoon salt
150 g white chocolate, coarsely chopped
75 g walnut pieces

Melt the white chocolate in the double saucepan over boiling water until smooth. Remove from the heat. Beat the egg yolks with the sugar in the Magimix until thick. Bring the cream and the milk to the boil. Beat half this mixture with the egg yolks. Transfer to the saucepan and stir in the remaining cream. Gradually mix with the white chocolate and vanilla. Cook slowly for five minutes but do not let the custard boil. Remove from the heat and strain the custard into a plastic container. Cool, stir from time to time. Freeze until mushy, beating occasionally. Fold in whipped cream, cover and freeze until needed.

Make the cookies. In a bowl, cream the butter and sugars together and beat in the egg and vanilla. Sieve the flour, baking powder and salt together into a bowl and lightly fold into the butter mixture. Carefully stir in the white chocolate and nuts. Place spoonfuls of the mixture on to a non-stick tin and bake for ten minutes or until the cookies are just golden. Cool for one minute and place on a wire rack to finish cooling. Store in an air-tight container. Makes approx 24 cookies.

SUMMER BBQ AND BUFFET FOR TWENTY

Surprise your guests with your inventiveness by making up ice cubes and place in each one a little borage flower and freeze. Float these in large glasses of Pimms or wine cup. Don't forget to get the BBQ going well before everybody arrives, there is nothing worse than waiting around endlessly for raw sausages and I am sure I needn't warn you of the all too frequent cases of food poisoning from undercooked meat or meat left out in the sun. Keep what food you are not BBQ-ing in the fridge, this will help to avoid salmonella and nasty bugs.

BBQ Menu
Serves 10

       Cold tomatoes stuffed with pine nuts, rice and chorizo
*   BBQ trout with potatoes, onions and paprika
*   A continental salad and walnut oil vinaigrette
*   Button mushrooms in pesto sauce
       Hazelnut and carrot cake
*   Exotic fruit salad in rosewater syrup

Wine: French Country Wine, 1989 Domaine de Rieux,
Vin de Pays des Côtes de Gascogne (throughout)

You can easily double the recipes for the tomatoes and trout, increase the salads according to your numbers and by having these two puddings you automatically have enough for up to 20 people. You can make the cake, stuffed tomatoes and mushroom salad the day before. The fruit salad is nicer if freshly made that morning. Leaving only the trout and salad to do at the last minute.

Buffets have a habit of being overloaded with food. All you need to plan for are two different types of main course, three salads and two kinds of puddings, usually one rich chocolate one and a light fruit dessert for those without a sweet tooth. Always keep the savoury food with its plates and cutlery away from the pudding plates and cutlery, otherwise people concentrating on chatting rather than the food will get into a muddle.

Now is your chance for a majestic central flower display. Lovely bright colours in summer and dark warm colours in winter with corresponding candles and napkins unless you use smart white linen.

Summer Buffet Menu

*   Cold sirloin of beef with mustard sauce
*   Smoked chicken and Caribbean salad
     New potatoes
*   Artichoke bottoms in pink peppercorn vinaigrette
*   A good mixed salad
*   Grown up lychee and lime jelly
     Chocolate and raspberry gâteau

Wine: *French Country Wine, 1988 Domaine Dusseau, Cabernet*
         Sauvignon, Vin de Pays d'Oc
         Hock, 1985 Oppenheimer Sackträger, Riesling Auslese,
         Weingut Louis Guntrum

You can make both the puddings the day before and cover with clingfilm until the last minute when you put them on the buffet table. Also make the artichoke salad and cook the beef if you want to the day before. Then all you have to do is make up the chicken dish. Cook plenty of potatoes and double up on the salad and vinaigrette a couple of hours before the party begins.

*Against **all** odds the English will BBQ!*

Cold Tomatoes Stuffed with Pine Nuts, Rice and Chorizo

Serves 10-12

I enjoy spicy, aromatic food which is why I enjoy eating these tomatoes. These are rather good served hot in winter with garlic bread.

Set oven at 180 C, 375 F, Gas Mark 4

> 10-12 beef tomatoes, washed and dried
> 225 g rice, cooked, rinsed and drained
> 100 g pine nuts, toasted under grill
> 300 g sliced chorizo (Spanish sausages)
> Virgin olive oil
> 2 cloves garlic, crushed
> Fresh thyme
> Salt and pepper

Remove the tops of the tomatoes and scoop out the flesh and discard. Pat dry with kitchen paper. Season with a little salt and pepper. Place in an oiled ovenproof dish.

Mix the rice, nuts and sausage with the crushed garlic, thyme and olive oil to moisten. Fill each tomato with this mixture. Trickle olive oil over the tomatoes and sprinkle with more thyme and bake for ten minutes but to not let the tomatoes split.

Serve the tomatoes at room temperature with a little more olive oil sprinkled over them so that they glisten in the sun.

BBQ Trout with Potatoes, Onions and Paprika
Serves 10

This is a Fife special, always cooked on the BBQ in Yorkshire. The trout of course having been caught a few hours before by my brother in law, Andrew Fife.

180 C, 350 F, Gas Mark 4 or BBQ

> 10 trout
> 1 large onion, very finely sliced
> 3 tablespoons chopped parsley
> 10 medium potatoes, peeled
> 10 x 25 g knobs of butter
> 2 cloves garlic, crushed
> Salt, black pepper and paprika
> 3 tablespoons grated Pecorino cheese

Rinse and dry the trout. Cut ten large pieces of foil and lay the onions in the centre of each piece. Place the fish on top, finely slice the potatoes and layer them over the trout. Season with the garlic, salt, pepper and paprika. Dot with butter and sprinkle with Pecorino and parsley and wrap up tightly. Bake for three quarters of an hour or until the potatoes and onions are soft, or BBQ.

Walnut Oil Vinaigrette
Enough for a salad for 8 - 12

1 teaspoon Dijon mustard
1 tablespoon Balsamic vinegar
Salt and pepper
1 teaspoon caster sugar
4 or 5 tablespoons walnut oil according to your taste preference
Fresh herbs as required

In a small bowl mix the mustard, seasoning, herbs and sugar and gradually incorporate the vinegar. Whisk or beat in the oil a little at a time until you have a glossy thick vinaigrette to toss your salad in.

A Continental Salad
Serves 10

The walnut oil vinaigrette makes this salad totally individual and distinctive and you can sprinkle fresh herbs over the salad in summer.

115 g baby sweetcorn, trimmed and halved
4 firm tomatoes, trimmed and sliced
$^1/_2$ cucumber peeled and sliced
125 g red chicory, trimmed and halved
15 g roquette, cleaned and dried
1 bunch of watercress, washed and trimmed
1 whole frisée salad, washed and trimmed
1 whole radicchio, washed and trimmed
Any fresh herbs

Mix all the ingredients together in a big salad bowl and toss in the walnut oil vinaigrette.

Button Mushrooms in Pesto Sauce
Serves 10

Cold in summer or hot in winter with garlic bread, this is delicious with freshly grated Parmesan or Romano cheese.

    1.6 kg fresh button mushrooms
    190 g jar pesto sauce
    Black pepper
    Grated Parmesan
    Olive oil

Wipe the mushrooms, clean and trim if necessary. Blanch the mushrooms in boiling salted water and drain. Pat dry with a cloth and transfer to a salad bowl. Mix in as much pesto sauce as you like, black pepper and cheese. Chill until needed.

Toss the mushrooms in extra olive oil as the pesto is usually rather thick.

Hazelnut and Carrot Cake

Serves 10

You can keep this cake un-iced in an airtight container for several days before you need it.

Set oven at 180 C, 350 F, Gas Mark 4

450 g carrots, topped and tailed
2 lemons
300 g hazelnuts with skins
6 eggs
300 g caster sugar
100 g plain flour
1 heaped teaspoon baking powder
2 heaped teaspoons ground mixed spice
450 g cream cheese
$^1/_2$ teaspoon vanilla essence
100 g icing sugar, sifted

Grease and line a deep fruit cake tin. Peel and grate the carrots and the rind of one of the lemons. Chop the hazelnuts in a food processor. Separate the eggs, place the yolks and sugar together and whisk until pale. Stir in the nuts, carrots and lemon rind and juice of one lemon. Fold in the flour, baking powder and mixed spice. Whisk the egg whites until stiff and fold into the cake mixture and spoon into the tin. Bake the cake until golden and springy to the touch, for about 50 minutes. Cool in the tin before turning on to a rack.

To make the icing, mix together the cream cheese with the remaining grated lemon rind, vanilla essence and icing sugar and loosen it up with as much lemon juice as you like. Slit the cake in half and spread with one third of the mixture then put the cake back together again. Swirl the remaining cream cheese all over it. Scatter crystalized rose petals or violets over it and keep chilled until needed.

Exotic Fruit Salad in Rosewater Syrup
Serves 10

The delicate smell of Rosewater makes this fruit salad so special, in summer you can sprinkle fresh rose petals on the top at the last minute.

1 x 425 g tin Lotus sliced mango in light syrup
1 x 425 g tin Lotus lychees in natural juice
2 bananas, peeled and sliced into the juice of $1/2$ lemon
10 fresh dates, halved and stones removed
1 star fruit, trimmed and sliced
3 ripe, kiwi fruit, peeled and sliced
225 g cleaned ripe blueberries, raspberries or strawberries
1 $1/2$ tablespoons Langdale's Essence of Rosewater
200 g box Amaretti di Saronno Lazzaroni biscuits to serve

Serve with crème chantilly (page 61).

Mix all the fruit, syrup and Rosewater together in a pretty glass bowl and chill for a few hours. Serve with the biscuits and crème chantilly. To increase the quantity to serve at a buffet for example, include 225 g of each of the soft fruit suggested.

Cold Sirloin of Beef with Mustard Sauce
Serves 10

This recipe is super for buffets or post-theatre dinners as you can leave everything perfectly prepared before you go out.

Set oven at 200 C, 400 F, Gas Mark 6

> 1.6 kg boned sirloin of beef
> Olive oil
> Crushed garlic
> Thyme
> 1 bunch watercress
>
> *Mustard sauce*
> 300 ml dry white wine
> 1 bay-leaf
> $^1/_2$ teaspoon crushed black peppercorns
> $^1/_4$ teaspoon fresh thyme
> 4 tablespoons tarragon vinegar
> 2 shallots, finely chopped
> 4 heaped teaspoons Dijon mustard
> 8 tablespoons whipping cream
> 2 tablespoons chopped chives

In a roasting tin, sear the beef on all sides and both ends in olive oil, garlic and thyme. Move the beef to the oven and cook for 45 minutes. Cool and chill.

Make the sauce: reduce the white wine, bay-leaf, peppercorns, thyme, vinegar and shallots in a saucepan until only half remains. Strain, set aside and cool. In a mixing bowl, blend the mustard, cream, the reduction and chives. Slice the meat into very thin slices. Decorate with the watercress and serve with the mustard sauce.

Smoked Chicken and Caribbean Salad
Serves 20

This is really just a glorified version of coronation chicken but the combination of flavours and textures that I have put together are much more fun.

        2 kg Easy Cook American rice
        2 large smoked chickens, cut up into small pieces
        800 g French mayonnaise
        Juice of 1 lemon
        2 tablespoons Worcestershire sauce
        Few shakes of Tabasco
        345 g jar mango chutney
        3 ripe bananas, peeled and sliced
        2 ripe mangoes, peeled and sliced
        822 g tin of pineapple chunks, drained
        200 g large cashew nuts
        450 g baby sweetcorns, trimmed and halved
        Salt and pepper
        Cayenne pepper

Blanch the sweetcorn in boiling water. Drain and refresh under cold water.
In a big bowl mix the mayonnaise with the lemon juice, Worcestershire sauce,
Tabasco and chutney. Slice all the chicken, fruit and vegetables into bite sized
pieces and mix into the mayonnaise. Season to taste with salt and pepper and
chill until needed.

Arrange the rice in a big circle on two very large meat dishes and spoon the
salad inside the ring. Sprinkle the cayenne over the salad and serve.

Artichoke Bottoms in Pink Peppercorn Vinaigrette
Serves 10

It is so nice to get a really different salad at a buffet or BBQ. I often prepare this recipe as a summer starter.

2 x 290 g jars artichoke bottoms
900 g button mushrooms, rinsed and dried
Walnut oil vinaigrette, (page 81)
Crushed garlic
4 tablespoons chopped parsley
85 g pink peppercorns

You can make this a day in advance.

Strain the artichokes and cut into slices. Slice the mushrooms finely and mix with artichokes. Mix the crushed garlic, parsley and pink peppercorns with the walnut vinaigrette. Toss the artichokes and mushrooms in the vinaigrette and chill until needed.

A Good Mixed Salad
Serves 10

A glossy, richly coloured and textured salad looks wonderful, cool and healthy in summer. In winter it cuts through the richness of our heavy food.

1 whole Batavia lettuce, washed and dried
1 whole Lollo Rosso lettuce, washed and dried
1 whole oak leaf lettuce, washed and dried
2 white chicory, trimmed and sliced
225 g button mushrooms, cleaned and trimmed
225 g fennel, trimmed and sliced
2 red peppers, trimmed and sliced
225 g yellow cherry tomatoes, halved
2 tablespoons chopped parsley

Tear up the lettuces into manageable pieces and combine with the remaining ingredients in a big salad bowl and toss with walnut oil vinaigrette, (page 81).

Grown-up Lychee and Lime Jelly

Children and adults will all love this tangy jelly. It is very refreshing in summer but definitely not to be thrown around the Nursery.

1 x 425 g tin Lotus lychees in syrup
2 x 142 g packets lime flavour jelly
Juice of 4 fresh limes
Grated rind of 2 fresh limes
More lychees or fresh mint to decorate

Lightly oil your jelly ring mould. Boil 600 ml of water, pour on to the jelly and stir until dissolved. Drain the lychees and pat dry on absorbent paper. Grate the limes into the jelly and then add the juice. Pour the jelly into the mould and chill in the deep freeze for speed.

When the jelly has thickened enough to hold the lychees, place them attractively in the jelly and leave to set. Keep the jelly chilled in the refrigerator until needed. Turn out on to a big plate and fill the middle with fresh or tinned lychees and sprigs of fresh mint and serve with cream or ice cream.

Chocolate and Raspberry Gâteau
Serves 10

The almonds and the jam in this recipe makes this gâteau much less chocolatey than you would expect and although it is very rich it is very moreish.

Set the oven at 190 C, 375 F, Gas Mark 5

> A little melted butter
> Bakewell paper
> 150 g plain chocolate
> 125 g unsalted butter
> 100 g caster sugar
> 100 g ground almonds
> 4 eggs, separated
> 50 g fresh brown breadcrumbs
> 3 tablespoons melted raspberry jam
> 300 g fresh raspberries, frozen raspberries in winter
> 450 ml double cream

Line the base of a spring release tin with Bakewell paper and brush with a little melted butter. Stir the chocolate over very low heat until melted. Remove from the heat. Cream the butter and sugar until light and fluffy. Stir in the almonds, egg yolks, breadcrumbs and chocolate.

Stiffly beat the egg whites and fold into the mixture. Pour into the tin and bake for 30 - 35 minutes until firm to touch. Leave to cool under a damp, clean cloth. Turn out the cake on to a wire rack and brush the cake with the jam. Whip the cream and spread all over the cake and decorate with the raspberries.

A good tip if using frozen raspberries is to put them on the cake at the last minute when they are semi-frozen so that the juices don't run into the cream.

A DINNER FOR THE
GLORIOUS TWELFTH

Serves 12

In London you have to book your grouse in advance for the Glorious Twelfth and any high class butcher will be able to get you some and have them plucked and drawn but at a price. Nothing should compete with the grouse so I suggest having a pudding and a savoury instead of a starter. This leaves you time to concentrate on the main course.

MENU

*	Roast grouse with gin and juniper berry sauce
	Spiced red cabbage and apple
*	Creamed potatoes (page 42)
	Amaretto and peach ice cream
*	Water chestnuts wrapped in bacon (page 13)

Wine: *Red Burgundy, 1985 Ch. de Chamirey, Mercurey, Marquis de Jouennes d'Herville*
Australia, 1988 Heggies Vineyard, Rhine Riesling, Botrytis Affected
Crusted Port, Churchill, bottled 1984

Peaches should be wonderfully full flavoured and ripe in August so buy them well in advance to make sure they are. Make this delicious ice cream and freeze it until needed. You can prepare the savoury any time during the day: cover and keep chilled until just before you start eating your pudding. Grill the water chestnuts while you clear away the pudding plates. You can make the red cabbage the day before and peel the potatoes and keep them in water until needed. Leaving only the grouse dish to prepare in the evening.

Spiced Red Cabbage and Apple
Serves 12

This dish freezes very well so it is ideal for entertaining but keeps equally well in the fridge for several days.

> 1 large onion, peeled and halved
> 50 g butter
> Salt and pepper
> $1/2$ teaspoon grated nutmeg
> $1/2$ teaspoon ground cloves
> 1 red cabbage, trimmed
> 4 tablespoons vinegar
> 2 tablespoons brown sugar
> 4 tablespoons water
> 3 tablespoons sultanas
> 2 cooking apples, peeled and sliced

Cut the onion into very fine slices and cook in butter until soft but not brown. Season with salt, pepper, nutmeg and cloves. Slice the cabbage and stir into the onions. Sprinkle with vinegar, sugar, water, sultanas and lastly the apple. Stir regularly over medium heat for about 20 minutes or more.

Roast Grouse with Gin and Juniper Berry Sauce
Serves 6

The Glorious Twelfth is here at last. If you are lucky enough to be in Scotland at the time, here is a super recipe to try.

Set oven at 200 C, 400 F, Gas Mark 6

> 12 rashers rindless bacon
> 6 grouse, plucked and drawn
> 100 g butter
> Salt, pepper and thyme
> Olive oil
> 2 bay-leaves
> 1 onion, peeled and finely sliced
> 18 juniper berries, crushed
> 150 ml gin
> 200 ml chicken or game stock
> 50 g butter, in tiny bits
> 6 slices brown bread, crusts removed
> Lard or oil for frying bread

Clean and dry the birds and wrap each one in two slices of bacon and spread with butter, salt, pepper and thyme. Lay all the onions and bay-leaves in the bottom of a roasting tin and sprinkle with oil, salt, pepper and thyme. Place the grouse on top of them with the juniper berries. Roast in the oven for ten minutes and then baste the birds. Add the game stock and mix with the onions and juniper berries and roast for another 20 minutes or until crispy on the outside and pink inside.

Remove the birds from the pan and ladle off any excess fat. Scrape around the tin over a high heat, pour in the gin and boil for two minutes. Strain the sauce into a saucepan and simmer over low heat. Adjust the seasoning and stir in the butter, piece by piece until the sauce is thick and glossy.

Meanwhile fry the bread in the fat and drain on absorbent paper. Place a grouse on each piece and on to each plate. Pour over the sauce and serve immediately.

Grouse with Gin

Amaretto and Peach Ice Cream
Serves 16

This quantity makes enough for a couple of small dinner parties so keep the ice cream sealed and prepare enough peaches to freeze for another time.

> 700 g ripe peaches, peeled and sliced
> 225 g caster sugar
> Juice of 1 lemon
> 175 g crumbled Amaretti (baby macaroons)
> 3 tablespoons Amaretto di Saronno
> 6 large egg yolks
> 568 ml double cream
> 284 ml whipped cream
> 16 fresh peaches, peeled and poached in rosé wine, sugar and lemon rind
>   until soft but firm.

Halve the 16 poached peaches and remove the stones. Serve in a crystal bowl in the syrup or freeze in two containers.

Make the ice cream. Beat the eggs and the sugar in the Magimix until light and creamy. Bring the double cream to the boil and pour into the Magimix beating all the time. Cook the custard over low heat until thick, do not boil. Liquidize the 700 g of peaches with the lemon juice and Amaretto and stir into the custard. Cool and then freeze.

Beat the custard occasionally. When the ice cream is nearly frozen fold in the whipped cream and amaretti and return to the freezer. This is best sealed and left overnight.

Serve the ice cream with the poached peaches either in separate crystal bowls or on individual plates, together with Askeys De-Luxe Chocolate Curls.

A HALLOWEEN OR FIREWORKS PARTY

Halloween is a chance to go to the local joke shop and buy lots of spooky decorations, there are marvellous fake spider's webs and beastly black spiders! Black candles and carved out pumpkins with candles inside add lots of atmosphere and perhaps a party game or two; 'Murder in the Dark' for instance is a good idea.

Most of us love fireworks and if I can organise a party at home I do. Lots of sparklers and mulled wine around a big bonfire and a very safe and carefully arranged firework display is such fun for everybody. Handing around those delicious hot sausages in honey and tarragon on page 12 keeps everyone warm and cheerful.

MENU

Pumpkin soup with sage croûtons
Moroccan Lamb Couscous
Aromatic Carrots with cloves
Toffee crunch ice cream

Make the ice cream the day before and freeze until needed. You can do almost everything else the day before too. Carve out a big pumpkin and clean it thoroughly to serve the soup in at the party. It is also a very effective and eyecatching centre piece for any halloween party. Keep the pumpkin in a cool place overnight then make the soup with the scooped out flesh so it is ready to heat through, followed by the casserole. Then all you need to prepare are the vegetables a couple of hours before dinner.

I suggest you find a good recipe for mulled wine. Do make sure you use the cheapest red wine possible!

Pumpkin Soup with Sage Croûtons
Serves 8

Just for fun, carve out a large pumpkin and serve the soup in it for Halloween or a fireworks party. Scrape out the flesh, remove the pith and seeds and follow the recipe below.

> 1 medium whole pumpkin or
> 398 ml tinned pumpkin
> 50 g butter
> 1 large onion, finely chopped
> 50 g flour
> Salt, pepper, nutmeg and mace
> Ground cinnamon, cloves and ginger
> 1 litre chicken stock
> 300 ml orange juice
> 1 teaspoon sugar
> 142 ml double cream
> 2 tablespoons chopped parsley
> 8 slices white bread, finely cubed
> Sage
> Oil

Melt the butter and slowly cook the onion until transparent. Meanwhile, cut the pumpkin into small pieces, peel off the skin and remove the pith and seeds. Add the pumpkin to the onion and stir in the flour, cook for a minute while you add the salt, pepper, nutmeg and mace. Mix in half a teaspoon of each of the ground cinnamon, cloves and ginger. Cover with stock and simmer for 35 minutes. Cool the soup. Liquidize with the orange juice and return to the saucepan. Fill the liquidizer with a little water and swill round and pour into the saucepan, stir in one teaspoon of sugar and correct seasoning.

Reheat the soup and serve with swirls of cream and a sprinkling of parsley. Fry the croûtons in the oil with a little chopped or rubbed sage. Dry on absorbent paper and serve with the soup.

Moroccan Lamb Couscous
Serves 8-10

Set oven at 190 C, 375 F, Gas Mark 5

3 tablespoons olive oil
3 large onions, peeled and sliced
1.4 kg lamb neck fillets, in thick slices
1 large swede, peeled and cubed
salt and pepper
250 g dried apricots
250 g pitted prunes
1 large red pepper, ends and seeds removed
2 cloves garlic, peeled and crushed
3 heaped tablespoons tomato paste
397 g tin chopped tomatoes
1 level teaspoon each of ground cloves and cinnamon
$^1/_2$ teaspoon each grated nutmeg and coriander seeds
3 cardamom pods, seeds only
pinch of cayenne pepper, (according to taste)
300 ml red wine

In a large casserole, heat the oil and cook the onions until nearly soft, add the lamb and swede and brown for a few minutes then add all the remaining ingredients in the given order. Mix thoroughly, cover with a lid and bake in the oven for about an hour. Check there is enough liquid half way through the cooking time. You can top it up with water, wine or stock.

500 g Groult medium grain couscous
pinch of saffron strands
3 tablespoons olive oil
3 tablespoons of butter
Salt and pepper

To make the couscous, pour one litre of water into a large saucepan and add the oil and one teaspoon of salt and bring to the boil. Remove from the heat, add couscous and saffron and allow it to swell for three to five minutes. Add the butter and pepper and heat on a very low hob for a further three to five minutes, separating the grains with a fork. Serve immediately with the lamb casserole.

Toffee Crunch Ice Cream

Serves 12-14

This is one of the easiest and most delicious ice creams I have ever made and certainly a favourite with children and grown-ups alike.

> 1 litre double cream, lightly whipped
> 3 x 405 g tins condensed milk
> 75 g digestive biscuits, crumbled up

Boil the tins of condensed milk unopened for three hours in water. I usually put a bit of foil at the bottom of the pan and a slice of lemon rind in the water to prevent discolouring the pan. Keep water level over the tins so they cook evenly. When they are cold, open them and gently mix blobs into the cream. Carefully fold in the biscuits and freeze until needed. Soften slightly before serving with butterscotch sauce, (page 166).

A SPECIAL COLLECTION OF MY FAVOURITE RECIPES

STARTERS

Cream of Mussel and Saffron Soup
Serves 6

By using frozen mussels you save hours and hours of scrubbing, tugging and washing these obstinate molluscs.

> 454 g frozen mussels, defrosted
> 100 g diced carrots
> 50 g diced shallots
> 100 g butter
> 50 g plain flour
> Generous pinch of saffron
> 1 teaspoon caster sugar
> 1 teaspoon fresh dill, chopped
> 300 ml double cream
> Salt and pepper
> 300 ml white wine
> 600 ml water
> A little freshly chopped parsley

Sauté the carrots and shallots in the butter in the pan. When the vegetables are slightly soft stir in the flour, saffron, dill, sugar and seasoning. Gradually stir in the wine and the water. Stir occasionally and simmer for 20 minutes. Add the mussels to the soup and bring to the boil immediately. Reduce the heat and pour in the cream. Stir for a few minutes. Reheat the soup before serving, sprinkled with parsley and accompany with crusty French bread.

Camembert en Croûte

Serves 4

This is delicious as a light lunch with a crisp green salad.

Set oven at 190 C, 375 F, Gas Mark 5

300 g packet frozen filo pastry leaves
3 large, thin slices prosciutto (or 6 slices pre-packed)
One 270 g Camembert, chilled
Black pepper
50 g melted butter
265 g jar luxury cranberry sauce with Port
1-2 tablespoons Port

Lay out four or more sheets of the pastry on top of each other, on a clean board. Wrap all the prosciutto around the cheese. Season with a little pepper and wrap up in the pastry. Pour one third of the butter into a baking tray and set the cheese on it. Brush the pastry with one third of the melted butter. Bake for ten minutes and brush with the other one third of butter and continue to bake for another ten minutes until golden brown. Remove from the oven and cool for ten minutes before serving with the cranberry sauce.

To serve the cranberry sauce heat with a little Port and serve.

Tagliolini with Goat's Cheese and Rosemary

Serves 4-6

250 g fresh tagliolini
2 tablespoons olive oil
Salt and black pepper
350 g courgettes, trimmed
2 small red peppers, trimmed
4 tablespoons extra virgin olive oil
2 cloves garlic, crushed
1 branch fresh rosemary
Juice of 2 lemons
200 g any goat's cheese

Finely slice the courgettes and peppers and cook briefly in salted boiling water, drain and refresh under cold water. Heat the two tablespoons olive oil in a saucepan and sauté the garlic with the rosemary, courgettes and peppers. After a couple of minutes add the lemon juice and mix well. Simmer for a minute or two and then remove from the heat.

Cook the pasta in boiling, salted water until al dente. Drain and transfer to a large warm bowl. Toss it in two tablespoons of the extra virgin olive oil with some salt and black pepper. Stir in the courgettes, peppers and juices. Slice up the goat's cheese and scatter over the pasta. Sprinkle with the remaining oil and serve immediately.

Fennel and Pine Nut Spaghetti
Serves 8

A good hint for cooking pasta is to add a little olive oil to the boiling water. This prevents the pasta from sticking together during cooking.

100 g Epicure pine kernels
100 g fresh grated Parmesan cheese
Approx 650 g fennel, trimmed and sliced
500 g spaghetti
Juice of two lemons
300 ml double cream
3 egg yolks
100 g butter
1 clove crushed garlic, salt and pepper
50 g fresh basil, chopped
50 g fresh parsley, chopped
Extra butter

Cook the fennel in boiling water until soft and drain. Toast the pine nuts under the grill for a few seconds. Cook the spaghetti in salted boiling water and drain. Return the spaghetti to its pan and dot with the extra butter, salt and pepper and toss once or twice. Keep covered until needed. Now mix the cream with the egg yolks in a small bowl and keep near at hand.

Melt the 100 g butter in another big saucepan, stir in the fennel and pine nuts and sauté briefly. Add the garlic, basil and parsley followed by the lemon juice, salt and pepper. Turn down the heat and stir in the cream mixture and transfer the pasta to this saucepan. Mix thoroughly over a low heat with the grated Parmesan.

Spoon the pasta into a warm china bowl and serve immediately. This is ideal for lunch with a fresh salad. You can serve more Parmesan cheese separately.

Quail and Grape Salad

Serves 4

If you feel the recipe is too extravagant, use two quail for four people; it will be just as delicious and impressive.

Set oven at 200 C, 400 F, Gas Mark 6

> 4 quail
> Olive oil
> Salt, pepper and thyme
> 2 glasses white wine
> 275 g bunch seedless green grapes
> 50 g Lambs lettuce, washed and trimmed
> Extra oil and white wine vinegar

Mix the oil with the salt, pepper and thyme and spoon it over the quail. Add the wine and roast in a hot oven until cooked but still pink. Clean and dry the grapes, cut in halves and arrange with slices of quail breast and the crispy legs on the lambs lettuce.

Add a little extra olive oil and wine vinegar to the pan juices and pour over each salad. Serve immediately.

Stewed Squid with Peas

Serves 6

The squid is delicious with wild rice as a main course or on its own as a hot starter.

2.27 kg whole squid, or 1 kg cleaned squid
4 tablespoons olive oil
2 cloves garlic, crushed
2 medium onions, finely sliced
3 tablespoons chopped parsley
2 tablespoons tomato paste
907 g frozen peas
Salt and fresh black pepper
225 ml red wine
Marjoram

Pull out the insides of the squid and squeeze out the juices. Throw away the head and tentacles and cut into medium sized pieces. Fry the onions in the oil until soft but not brown. Stir in the garlic, marjoram, peas and squid and cook for three minutes. Add the tomato paste and red wine, season to taste. Simmer for 15 minutes until tender and sprinkle with parsley.

Ragoût of King Prawns and Oyster Mushrooms

Serves 4

I don't need any excuses to use as much garlic as possible in everything I cook but garlic does go particularly well with prawns and mushrooms. So you can afford to be very generous with it in this recipe.

8-12 king prawns, washed
225 g oyster mushrooms, wiped
225 g flat mushrooms, wiped
1 tablespoon butter
1 tablespoon olive oil
Plenty of garlic, crushed
Juice of $1/2$ lemon
150 ml dry sherry
Salt and pepper
1 tablespoon chopped parsley
100 g butter

Melt the tablespoon of butter with the oil and garlic and add the prawns. Sauté until the shells are pink and the flesh inside is white. Meanwhile cut the mushrooms into manageable pieces and sauté for a few minutes in the 100 g butter. Add the sherry, lemon juice and parsley to the mushrooms and simmer for a few minutes.

Meanwhile peel the prawns, leaving on the tails and add them to the mushrooms and simmer for a couple of minutes. Correct the seasoning.

Serve the ragoût of prawns on four warm plates with fresh warm plain or garlic bread.

Grilled Tuna Fish Steaks with Capers and Tomatoes

Serves 4

Fresh tuna has gained in popularity now and makes tinned tuna fish seem rather uninteresting in comparison, although very useful for standbys and essential for salade niçoise.

        4 tuna fish steaks
        1 small onion
        1 bay-leaf
        4 tablespoons olive oil
        Salt and pepper
        Plenty of marjoram
        Plenty of garlic, crushed
        Juice of 1 lemon
        2 tablespoons capers in vinegar
        4 tomatoes, skinned and deseeded
        1 tablespoon chopped parsley

Mix the onion, bay-leaf, olive oil, salt and pepper, marjoram and garlic together in a bowl and marinate the tuna steaks for an hour or so. Discard the onion and bay-leaf. Turn the grill up very high and brush the fish with the marinade and grill until cooked through.

Place the tuna steaks on warm plates and cut the tomatoes in strips. Transfer the leftover marinade and lemon juice to a small saucepan and quickly heat through with the tomatoes and capers. Spoon the hot sauce over the fish, sprinkle with chopped parsley and serve.

Ricotta Tortelloni with Monkfish and Basil Sauce

Serves 6

350 g fresh ricotta tortelloni
700 g Monkfish, off the bone
1 large bunch basil leaves, chopped
100 g butter
1 glass demi-sec white wine
30 g chopped chives
Salt and black pepper
6 tablespoons double cream
A few extra chopped chives for decoration

Warm the plates first. Boil the pasta in salted water until al dente, about 12 minutes. Chop the Monkfish into bite sized cubes and cook in the butter for a few minutes. Pour over the glass of wine, basil and chives, add salt and pepper to taste and turn down the heat to simmer for a couple of minutes.

Lift out the fish and keep warm on a plate. Reduce the liquid by half and add the cream. Briefly cook the Monkfish in the sauce. Drain the pasta and carefully combine with the sauce and fish and heat through for a couple of minutes.

Carefully divide the pasta, Monkfish and sauce between the six plates and serve immediately sprinkled with a few chopped chives.

A Tasty French Tart

Warm Langoustine Tart

Serves 6

Set oven at 190 C, 375 F, Gas Mark 5

454 g packet shortcrust pastry
225 g peeled langoustines
2 courgettes, trimmed and thinly sliced
175 g fresh spinach, washed and trimmed
300 g tomatoes
4 eggs
225 g strained Greek yoghurt
1 bunch chives, cleaned and chopped
A few strands of saffron
Flour
Salt, pepper, thyme and grated nutmeg
Cayenne

Grease and flour a very large quiche or flan dish. Roll out the pastry on a floured surface, line the dish, trim neatly and prick the bottom of the pastry. Arrange the langoustines in the pastry case. Blanch and drain the courgettes and the spinach separately. Pat the spinach dry on kitchen paper. Meanwhile put the tomatoes in a bowl of boiling water and prick them. Leave for a few minutes and then remove their skins and discard the seeds. Slice up the flesh for the tart.

Arrange the spinach, courgettes and tomatoes over the langoustines. Now beat the eggs, yoghurt, chives, saffron together with the salt, pepper, thyme and grated nutmeg. Spoon the mixture over the vegetables. Sprinkle with cayenne and bake for 40 minutes until firm to touch and golden brown.

Crab Cakes with Chilli Sauce

Serves 8

I was staying in Maryland for Easter 1991 and my charming host and hostess, Andy and Vicky, made these wonderful melt-in-the-mouth crab cakes, a local traditional fish cake.

454 g frozen crab meat, thawed and drained
450 g potatoes, cooked and mashed
50 ml double cream
25 g butter
1 tablespoon chopped fresh parsley
Juice of half a lemon
Salt and pepper
A pinch of cayenne pepper
3 eggs, beaten
225 g fresh breadcrumbs
Vegetable oil for frying
300 g jar of tomato and chilli relish
Few drops of chilli sauce
Frisée lettuce and radicchio to decorate
Flour for dusting

Mix the crab with the potatoes, cream, butter, parsley, lemon juice, seasoning and cayenne. Chill for 20 minutes in the deep freeze and then spoon the mixture on to a floured board, forming the mixture into 16 crab cakes. Coat them with egg and breadcrumbs.

Heat the oil in a frying pan until very hot, add the fish cakes and fry, turning once until crisp and golden. Drain on absorbent kitchen paper. Add chilli sauce to the tomato and chilli relish. Serve with the crab cakes. Decorate each plate with a little frisée lettuce and radicchio and serve immediately.

Chilled Ceviche and Radicchio Salad

Serves 6

This traditional Mexican fish dish which is marinated raw fish, is clean and fresh tasting, ideal for figure conscious hostesses!
The salmon makes the dish colourful and attractive.

> 500 g salmon fillet, skinned
> 500 g cod fillet, skinned
> 8 juicy limes
> 1 teaspoon salt
> A few chilli seeds
> 1 large clove crushed garlic
> $^1/_2$ tablespoon coriander seeds
> Lots of black pepper
> A little coconut milk, optional
> 1 frisée lettuce or radicchio trimmed and washed

Remove any visible fish bones and cut all the fish into small cubes. Put the fish into a big dish and grate the rind of two of the limes over the fish. Squeeze the juice from all the limes and pour over the salmon and cod. Sprinkle with salt, chilli, crushed garlic, coriander seeds and black pepper. Leave to marinate for at least four hours in the fridge. Toss the fish from time to time. You can add a little coconut milk at the end if you like.

Dry the lettuce and radicchio and break up into attractive pieces. Serve the ceviche on the salad either in a large flat dish or on individual plates.

Pheasant, Orange and Chestnut Casserole
Serves 6

The deep freeze groans under the weight of last year's pheasants let alone the new season's bag which gets hurled in with less and less enthusiasm. So here is another recipe for you to try.

225 g smoked streaky bacon, cut into strips
Olive oil
2 medium sized onions, thinly sliced
2 medium carrots cut into small cubes
300 ml white wine
Finely grated zest of 1 orange
Salt and pepper and nutmeg
A large sprig of fresh thyme
2 pheasants, all bitter yellow fat removed
300 ml orange juice
300 ml chicken stock
450 g tin whole chestnuts
1 tablespoon cornflour in water
1 tablespoon chopped parsley

In a big casserole, fry the bacon in just enough oil to prevent sticking. As soon as the bacon fat starts to run add the onions, carrots and thyme and cook for a few minutes. Add the wine, orange zest and seasoning.

Now place the two pheasants on top of the vegetables and pour over the orange juice and stock. Cover the casserole and cook gently for 20 minutes. Turn the pheasants on to their other side and add the chestnuts. Simmer for a further 20 minutes or until the birds are tender.

Lift the birds out of the casserole and carve the breasts and arrrange the legs in a deep ovenproof dish or meat plate. Bring the sauce to boil over high heat and stir in the cornflour mixed with a little cold water, stir until thick and glossy. Spoon the sauce over the pheasants and serve sprinkled with chopped parsley.

Pheasant and Wild Mushroom Risotto
Serves 8

Use as many different kinds of mushrooms as you can find - the stronger the flavour the better. Unfortunately wild mushrooms are hard to find but they can usually be ordered from your greengrocer who will go to Covent Garden Market at the crack of dawn.

2 pheasants - plucked, drawn and roasted
75 g butter
600 ml chicken or pheasant stock (cube)
1 large onion, finely sliced
250 g white rice
56 g dried cèpes
250 g button mushrooms, cleaned
150 g English oyster mushrooms
600 ml white wine and water
Salt, pepper and nutmeg
200 ml single cream
1 bunch fresh parsley, finely chopped
125 g freshly grated Parmesan
25 g butter

Remove all the meat from the pheasants and chop into small pieces. Melt the butter in a large saucepan or casserole and cook the onions until soft but do not brown. Stir in the rice and cover with stock and cook for 15 minutes. Stir in the pheasant and mushrooms and add the white wine, water and seasoning. Simmer for ten minutes. If at any point the rice becomes dry, add more wine, stock or water. Just before serving stir in the cream, 25 g butter, parsley and Parmesan cheese. You can serve some of the Parmesan separately if you wish.

Pheasant Rolls in Bacon and Thyme
Serves 4

Use the legs and thighs for a casserole. This is delicious with turkey or chicken breasts too.

Set oven at 190 C, 375 F, Gas Mark 5

> 4 pheasant breasts
> Butter
> Salt and pepper
> 200 g rashers rindless bacon
> Thyme
> 300 ml white wine
> 4 bay leaves

Wrap the length of each pheasant breast with the bacon. Sprinkle with salt, pepper and thyme. Lay each breast on a bay-leaf and dot with a knob of butter.

Bake in a buttered oven-proof dish with the white wine until the bacon is crispy and the pheasant is tender. This takes about 25 minutes. Serve immediately with the juices.

Chicken Breasts in Cumin and Tomato Sauce

Serves 8

This dish is colouful and aromatic, very light and healthy and delicious with the wild rice (page 51).

Set oven at 190 C, 375F, Gas Mark 5

8 chicken breasts
150 ml white wine
Salt, pepper and butter
50 g butter
1 onion, finely chopped
2 heaped teaspoons ground cumin
1 heaped teaspoon ground coriander
Salt and pepper

2 x 397 g tins chopped tomatoes
950 g fresh tomatoes, skinned
1 heaped teaspoon sugar
Fresh chopped parsley to decorate

Wrap each chicken breast in foil and moisten with a little wine, butter, salt and pepper and seal each package. Place them in an oven-proof dish and bake for 30 minutes.

In a saucepan melt 50 g butter and cook the onion slowly until soft. Stir in the spices, seasoning, tinned tomatoes amd sugar. Remove the seeds from the fresh tomatoes and dice them. Stir into the onions and simmer for 20 minutes. Unwrap the chicken and place on a warm serving dish. Pour the chicken juices into the tomato sauce. If it is still too thick, add a little more water. Liquidize the sauce and pour it over the chicken breasts. Sprinkle with parsley and serve.

Quail, Pea and Bacon Casserole

Serves 4

This is a very unusual recipe picked up from my travels in Umbria in 1990. However this is a very simplified version and freezes very well.

8 quail, cleaned
1 large onion, finely sliced
450 g frozen peas
225 g streaky, rindless bacon
2 tablespoons olive oil
50 g butter
Salt and pepper
2 cloves garlic, crushed
Fresh marjoram
500 g beef tomatoes, skins and seeds removed
8 tablespoons white wine

Rinse and dry the quail. Heat the oil in a big casserole and cook the onions and bacon for ten minutes before adding the garlic, marjoram and quail and brown for a couple of minutes. Add the butter, peas, salt and pepper. Cut the tomatoes into medium sized pieces and add with the wine to the casserole. Cover and cook for 30 minutes or so until the birds are tender.

Italian Meat Balls in Sage and Tomato Sauce

Serves 6

675 g lean minced beef
12 sage leaves, finely chopped
50 g butter
2 tablespoons olive oil
2 tablespoons Parmesan cheese, grated
Salt, pepper and nutmeg
Plain flour
2 x 440 g jars Ragu tomato and sliced mushroom pasta sauce
Few drops chilli sauce
150 g oyster mushrooms
Extra grated Parmesan cheese

Mix together the meat, sage, half the butter, Parmesan and seasoning. When well blended shape into small balls with floured hands. Heat the remaining butter and oil and fry the balls until golden brown, about seven minutes. Add the mushrooms. Meanwhile scrape out the jars of tomato sauce into a saucepan, you can swill them out with a little bit of water. Then add the few drops of chilli sauce. Heat this through and then pour on to the meat balls and mushrooms. Shake the pan over the heat until well mixed and serve immediately with extra Parmesan cheese.

Calves Liver with Grapes and Sauternes

Serves 2

Calves liver is such a delicacy that it must only be cooked for a few minutes so that it retains it's fine flavour and texture.

4 slices calves liver
50 g butter
1 tablespoon olive oil
Salt and black pepper
150 ml Sauternes
125 g seedless white grapes, washed and dried

Cut off any membrane from the liver, sauté for a few minutes in the oil and half the butter. Season with salt and pepper and pour over the Sauternes. Shake the pan over the heat. Lift out the liver and divide between two plates. Cut the grapes in half, add to the pan and shake over a high heat.

Stir in the remaining butter to make the sauce thicker and richer. Spoon the sauce over the liver and serve immediately.

I suggest you drink the rest of the Sauternes with your pudding or fresh fruit.

Venison Sausages, Steak and Mushroom Casserole
Serves 6

Serve this hearty winter casserole with spiced red cabbage and apple (page 91) and creamed potatoes (page 42). It can be frozen or made a day in advance like most casseroles.

> 450 g venison sausages
> 2 tablespoons olive oil
> 1 large onion, peeled and sliced
> 900 g venison steak, cubed
> Salt, pepper and nutmeg
> 1 bay-leaf
> 10 juniper berries, crushed
> Rosemary
> 300 ml red wine
> 350 g flat mushrooms, sliced
> 1 tablespoon cornflour, dissolved in water

Prick the sausages with a sharp knife, halve them and fry the sausages in one tablespoon of oil for five minutes. Add another tablespoon of oil, the onions and the venison and brown evenly. Season with salt, pepper, nutmeg, bay-leaf, juniper berries, rosemary and red wine. Stir in the mushrooms and cover the casserole. Simmer until tender for about two hours. Towards the end of cooking time stir in the cornflour to thicken the casserole.

Lamb Chops with Roquefort Butter
Serves 8

16 lamb chops
200 g butter, softened
100 g Roquefort cheese, softened
Fresh black pepper
Pinch of rosemary
Olive oil
Crushed garlic
Fresh mint to decorate

Mix the butter and the Roquefort with the black pepper. Shape the butter into 16 equal portions, wrap in clingfilm and freeze.

Heat the olive oil with the garlic and rosemary and fry or roast the chops in the olive oil until crispy but still pink. Serve the chops with a portion of butter on each one and decorate with a little mint.

Sauté of Veal, Pesto and Pasta Shells
Serves 8

Pesto is a delicious basil sauce which the Italians use a lot with pasta. Use fresh pasta whenever possible as it is so much quicker to cook and nicer to eat.

900 g veal escalopes
500 g pasta shells
100 g jar pesto sauce
3 tablespoons olive oil
Crushed garlic
Black pepper
Freshly grated Parmesan

Cut the veal into fine strips, removing any fat. Boil the pasta until al dente. Meanwhile sauté the veal in the oil and garlic. Drain the pasta and put it into a warm bowl, pour over the pesto sauce and mix in the veal. Toss it all together and sprinkle with the Parmesan and black pepper. Serve immediately.

Vaguely Vegetarian Lasagne
Serves 8

The thought of no meat fills me with horror, however this particular Lasagne is so delicious and economical for kitchen lunch or supper that I cook it quite often. Anyway for any like minded people the option of mince is included.

Set oven at 200 C, 400 F, Gas Mark 6

> Optional 700 g beef mince
> 250 g box no pre-cooking lasagne
> 2 red onions, peeled and chopped
> 397 g tin Sainsburys chopped tomatoes and herbs
> 690 g Grand Italia Sugocasa Tomato sauce
> 2 cloves garlic, crushed
> Salt and pepper
> Oregano
> 250 g grated Mozzarella cheese
> 2 x 450 g Greek strained yoghurt
> 907 g Bonduelle frozen leaf spinach spheres
> 2 tablespoons olive oil
> 450 g courgettes, cleaned and trimmed
> 450 g button mushrooms, cleaned and trimmed
> Cayenne pepper

In a large saucepan heat the olive oil and gently cook the onions, when they are soft stir in the garlic, chopped tomatoes and sauce. Season to taste with salt, pepper and oregano. At this point add the mince if you are going to and simmer for 20 minutes. Meanwhile cook the spinach and drain. Slice and cook the courgettes and blanch the mushrooms, keeping all the vegetables separate. To put the lasagne together, spread some of the tomato (and mince) sauce over the bottom of the dish and cover with a layer of pasta. Spoon the courgettes over the pasta, add more sauce, followed by the mushrooms, the remaining tomato sauce and the spinach and one more layer of pasta. Finally add the Greek yoghurt and grated cheese. Sprinkle with cayenne pepper and bake for 35-40 minutes.

What to Drink With Impossible Food

The problem with cooks writing cookbooks, is that they have one track minds. Food, food, food - that's all they ever think about. As a result you will find - even in this cookbook - recipes for dishes that will make your toes go curly with pleasure, but which make your average wine merchant in the street tear his hair out with frustration.

'Take seventeen bars of chocolate...' they will say, or 'prepare a vinaigrette with the zest of a pound of fraises des bois...', quite impervious to the fact that, although delicious in their own right, this is 'impossible food' - dishes that will kill a wine stone dead. You will cook them, your guests will praise you to the skies, and you will get that warm glow of contentment that only comes when you know that you have been particularly clever, but the wine you have spent a small fortune on will be the one blot on an otherwise perfect evening. Disgruntled, you will go to bed resolving to give your wine merchant hell the next day or - even more frightening - never go to him again.

The problem with impossible food is that it's very often irresistibly delicious. The answer is to realise when you are cooking impossible food, and instead of serving a wine that will never cope, think creatively instead.

Chocolate is notoriously impossible. People have tried all sorts of combinations - Sauternes, Chablis, even Claret - but without much success except to those with terminally warped tastebuds. To my mind, the only really safe option is to take a leaf out of Monsieur Suchard's book and head for the spirits cupboard. Here you can be really creative. For the seriously sweet toothed, liqueurs offer a wealth of possibilities - think of your favourite liqueur chocolate and quadruple it. Cointreau, Cherry Brandy, Grand Marnier, Bailey's Irish Cream - it all depends on what the pudding is based on. If all this seems too sickly, try one of the delicious Eaux de Vie Blanches from around the Black Forest - Mirabell from plums, Williams Birne from pears, Framboise from raspberries or Kirsch from cherries. If you have never tried them, just imagine your favourite fruit distilled down until all that remains is the essence. They are also seriously good poured over fruit salad....

Traditionalists will want to try Cognac, but for a change buy a bottle of Armagnac instead. Its fiery taste will cut through almost anything. Or a single malt whisky, or a top quality Calvados. See what I mean about creativity?

It is very difficult to be creative, however, when faced with vinegar, which is simply wine that has been allowed to go off. If you leave an opened bottle of wine, no matter how delicious, in a few days it will have changed into vinegar. If you want the process to happen a little faster, simply add a few drops of vinegar to the bottle, and wait a few moments. In exactly the same way, a dish that relies on vinegar for its flavour will make any wine you drink with it taste horrible. There is no clever way out of this as far as the wine is concerned, but you could always adopt the French solution, and substitute the vinegar in any recipe (and especially vinaigrette) with lemon juice.

Soup can also be impossible, especially if its very spicy. This is the time to resort to that under-rated and forgotten drink, Sherry. All sorts are delicious, as long as they're dry. Fino, obviously, but Manzanilla is a particular favourite of mine - Fino which has been matured in the bodegas of the coastal town of Sanlúcar de Barrameda, where the wind from the Atlantic gives the wine a delicious salty tang. Don't forget that all sherry is originally dry, and that it is possible to find superb Amontillado and even Oloroso which is light years away from the sticky concoctions we poor British have been subjected to, which is perfect for heavier soups. Keep a look out for Almacenista sherry - unblended, intense in flavour and how the Spanish drink sherry themselves. And, to be really Victorian, invest in a bottle of dry Madeira - Sercial, Verdelho or the inaccurately named Rainwater, and realise what you have been missing all these years. Madeira is also excellent with that other destroyer of wine, melon. Or you could try a glass of tawny Port, lightly chilled, as they drink it in Opporto.

Another excellent idea for starters is the favourite drink of the Cognac Producers, Pineau des Charentes. Essentially a lightly fortified sweet white wine, it has the extraordinary ability to completely cleanse the palate, so even if the first course is enough to blow your guests' socks off the rest of the meal won't suffer in comparison.

Eastern food is an especial problem. Hardly surprising, really - the cooking has developed for thousands of years without the cooks even knowing that wine existed. Alsatian wine often has the flavour to cope with spicy Chinese food - or drink tea like they do. And with Indian food there really is no alternative but beer - ice cold, if only to give your tastebuds a chance.

With all this 'impossible food', you have to think a little bit harder than you do in normal circumstances, and not feel constrained to wine, or to alcohol at all. If, though, convention gets the better of you and you simply must have a bottle of wine, for heaven's sake don't spend a fortune on it, or expect too much of it. Or ring me up and complain the next day.

MENUS FOR SHOOTING WEEKENDS

Roll on February is the cry of the shooting widow! If however you are the hostess then a meticulous campaign is ahead of you and should be planned down to the very last detail. Once you have your dates and guns organised the essential thing of course is not to give a regular gun the same menu twice. If everyone is arriving on Friday night then of course a good dinner has to be provided. I also find that as people are confronted by game solidly for the next three months, fish and seafood are ideal. So for Friday night I would suggest a menu as follows.

Friday Night Menu for Eight

Courgette and dill soup
*   Fillets of lemon sole with tomato and chive sauce
New potatoes
Mangetouts
Pear and vanilla cream tart

Wine: *Sherry, Choice Fino-Amontillado*
Australia, 1989 Rothbury Estate Chardonnay, Brokenback
 Vineyard
White Bordeaux, 1987 Ch. Roustit, Ste. Croix du Mont

You can make the soup and the tart on Friday morning leaving just the fish and vegetables for the evening. Saturday has to be very traditional, a huge cooked breakfast, of course, and for the shooting lunch perhaps a menu as shown overleaf.

Shooting Lunch for Eight

Old partridges in Madeira casserole
Spiced red cabbage and apple, (page 91)
*   Parsnip and swede purée
Baked potatoes
Nursery ginger and syrup pudding

Wine: *French Country Wine, 1989 Domaine de la Garenne,*
                Côtes du Ventoux
                The King's Ginger Liqueur

You can make the casserole and purée on Friday and heat through whilst you make the pudding and bake the potatoes on Saturday morning.

Once all the guests have come down from their hot baths in the evening they will be ready for a feast. This is the menu I often do for the shooting weekends that I cook for in Shropshire.

Dinner for Twelve
Serves 12

Mushroom and quails eggs en cocotte
Veal and hazelnut rolls in Grand Marnier and orange sauce
White chocolate profiteroles and dark chocolate sauce
Cheese and Port to follow

Wine: *California, 1988 Julius Wile Sauvignon Blanc, Napa Valley*
                Australia, 1984 Yalumba Signature Reserve, Cabernet/Shiraz,
                S. Smith & Sons
                Port, 1972 Taylor's Quinta da Vargellas

Once again the veal can be prepared on Friday and kept covered and chilled until needed. The profiteroles should be made on Saturday afternoon after lunch and the starter can be made early evening. However, if you are out shooting with your guests all day, I suggest you employ a cook!!

For Sunday breakfast I always produce grapefruit and lightly boiled eggs and toast to ease the hangovers. Lunch is usually a simple roast like lamb or beef with all the trimmings and my Hot Gooseberry Sponge pudding (page 136) and custard or my Banana and Rum Crumble (page 137), with cream; swiftly followed by any remains of last night's cheese and Port.

Courgette and Dill Soup

Serves 8

1 kg courgettes
1 small onion, peeled and sliced
1 tablespoon olive oil
$^3/_4$ litre chicken stock
1 heaped tablespoon cornflour
$^1/_2$ litre milk
300 ml single cream
1 bunch fresh dill
50 g butter
Extra cream and dill for decoration

Wash the courgettes, trim the ends and slice finely. Heat the oil and cook the onions gently until soft. Pour in the stock and cook for ten minutes until the cougettes are soft. Mix the cornflour with a little water and stir into the soup. Simmer for a couple of minutes then leave to cool. Liquidize the soup with the dill, milk and cream and transfer to a saucepan. Stir in the butter and simmer for a couple of minutes before serving with swirls of cream and a sprinkling of dill.

Fillets of Lemon Sole with Tomato and Chive Sauce

Serves 8

You can make this recipe with Dover Sole if you prefer but it is much more expensive and most people can't taste the difference.

> 1 large lemon sole fillet each
> 8 wedges of lemon
> Juice of 2 lemons
> 6 medium tomatoes
> 250 g unsalted butter
> 6 tablespoons medium dry sherry
> 6 tablespoons double cream
> 2 large bunches chives
> Salt and fresh ground black pepper

Blanch the tomatoes, skin and remove the seeds from them. Cut the flesh into strips. Grease a baking tray with 50 g of the butter to grill the fillets without them overlapping. Sprinkle four of them with salt and pepper, half the lemon juice and dot with half the butter between them. Grill for a few minutes and transfer on to warm plates. Proceed exactly the same way with the other four but keep all the fish juice as well.

To make the sauce place the baking tray over direct heat and bring the juices to boil, add the sherry and boil for one minute. Stir in the tomatoes and chives and continue to boil for another minute. Stir in the cream and after another minute or two the creamy sauce will thicken slightly. Divide spoonfuls of the sauce over the lemon sole and serve at once with wedges of lemon.

Pear and Vanilla Cream Tart
Serves 8

If you can't get ripe pears then simply cook them in a little syrup and proceed with the recipe.

Set oven at 200 C, 400 F, Gas Mark 6
Change down to 180 C, 350 F, Gas Mark 5

> 500 g packet fresh shortcrust pastry
> 3 small ripe pears, peeled and trimmed
> A little lemon juice
> 120 ml milk
> 120 ml double cream
> 1 teaspoon vanilla essence
> 4 eggs
> 175 g caster sugar
> 25 g caster sugar
> 1 teaspoon of flour

Grease and flour a large fluted flan dish. Roll out the pastry on a clean floured surface and line the flan dish. Cover with greaseproof paper and fill with ceramic balls to bake in the oven at the top temperature for 20 minutes until the edges are light brown.

Meanwhile bring the milk and cream to the boil and then add the vanilla essence. Beat the eggs with the 175 g of sugar in a food processor and pour in the cream and beat until smooth. Add the flour, whizz quickly and then transfer this mixture to a bowl. Slice the pears into fan shapes and sprinkle with lemon juice.

Remove the paper and ceramic balls from the pastry and arrange the pears in fan shapes around the base. Pour the cream custard over the pears and sprinkle with the remaining sugar. Bake for about 20 minutes or until set and golden. Serve warm or chilled.

Old Partridge in Madeira Casserole
Serves 8

If you are lucky enough to have young partridges I would undoubtably suggest that you enjoy them roasted following either the wood pigeon recipe (page 161) or the grouse recipe (page 92).

8 old partridges, plucked and drawn
100 g butter
2 large onions, peeled
450 g button mushrooms, cleaned and trimmed
113 g smoked ham, chopped
Plenty of thyme, salt and pepper
600 ml chicken or game stock
1 full wine glass Madeira
2 tablespoons cornflour in 150 ml water
4 slices brown bread, crusts removed
2 tablespoons chopped parsley
Extra oil

Very finely slice the onions. In a casserole, melt the butter over low heat and cook the onions until nearly soft. Brown the birds with the onions and then add the mushrooms. Season with the thyme, salt and pepper. Sauté for a few minutes with the Madeira and add the chopped ham and the stock. Put the lid over the casserole and simmer on low heat for one hour and 30 minutes until the birds are tender. Stir in the cornflour to thicken the sauce. Fry the bread in oil until crispy and cut in halves and keep warm.

Cut each bird in half with game scissors and arrange on a warm dish. Spoon all the sauce over, sprinkle with chopped parsley and arrange the halves of fried bread around the dish before serving.

Parsnip and Swede Purée

Serves 8

This is a delicious combination for duck and beef casseroles. You can make it in advance and reheat it in a low oven.

1 kg swede, peeled and chopped
1 kg parsnips, peeled and chopped
150 g soft butter
100 ml double cream
Plenty of grated nutmeg, salt and pepper

Cook both root vegetables in salted water until soft. Drain in a colander. Put half the quantity in a food processor and blend to a purée with the cream. Transfer this back to the saucepan. Now blend the remaining vegetables with the butter and mix into the purée in the saucepan. Season to taste. Reheat gently and then spoon into a warm serving dish. Cover with clingfilm until needed.

Nursery Ginger and Syrup Pudding
Serves 8

A hot and filling nursery pudding ideal for a Sunday lunch party in winter.

> 6 tablespoons of golden syrup
> 100 g margarine
> 100 g caster sugar
> 2 eggs, beaten
> 2 teaspoons ground ginger
> $^{1}/_{2}$ teaspoon mixed spice
> 175 g self-raising flour, sifted
> A little milk
> 3 tablespoons chopped ginger

Fill a saucepan with water and bring it to the boil. Grease a large pudding basin and spoon the syrup into the bottom. Cream the margarine and sugar together until pale and fluffy. Add the ground ginger, mixed spice and the eggs and beat briefly. Carefully fold in the flour and chopped ginger and add a little milk to make it into dropping consistency.

Pour the mixture into the pudding basin and cover with grease-proof paper making a pleat along the centre to allow for expansion. Secure with string and steam for two hours. Keep topping up the water.

Turn out the pudding on to a warm plate and serve with cream.

Mushroom and Quails Eggs en Cocotte
Serves 12

I have taken this wonderful idea from The Hon Mrs. L. Addington. I hope my version is as good as hers.

Set oven at 200 C, 400 F, Gas Mark 6

> 900 g flat mushrooms, sliced
> 1 teaspoon thyme
> 100 g butter
> Salt, pepper and nutmeg
> 2 dessertspoons sherry
> 225 g Greek strained yoghurt
> 24 quails eggs

> *Hollandaise sauce*

> 250 g butter
> 5 egg yolks
> 2 tablespoons lemon juice
> Salt and pepper

Cook the mushrooms and thyme in the butter until soft. Season, add the sherry and cool. Transfer to a food processor and finely chop the mixture and fold in the yoghurt. Spoon this mixture into 12 ramekins. Carefully break two quails eggs into each ramekin.

Hollandaise Sauce
Melt the butter until boiling. Place the egg yolks in the Magimix with the lemon juice and seasoning. Gradually pour in the butter beating the sauce all the time. When the sauce is thick, spoon it over the quails eggs and bake in a bain-marie for 15 minutes, so that the eggs are cooked and the Hollandaise slightly browned and puffy.

Veal and Hazelnut Rolls in Grand Marnier and Orange Sauce

Serves 12

It is a bit of a bore tying up the veal rolls but it makes them look very neat and professional. They can be made the day before and freeze well.

12 veal escalopes, thinly beaten out
1 onion, finely chopped
125 g butter
100 g hazelnuts, browned
Salt and pepper
1 teaspoon dried thyme
125 g brown breadcrumbs
Grated zest and juice of one orange
2 tablespoons oil
Grand Marnier
Coursely grated rind of 1 orange
Juice of 3 large oranges
1 tablespoon cornflour in 300 ml water
A couple of bunches of fresh thyme and an orange to decorate

Cook the onion in half the butter in a frying pan until soft. Grind the toasted hazelnuts coarsely in the magimix. Mix them with the onions. Add salt, pepper and thyme, cook for two minutes. Remove the pan from the heat and stir in the breadcrumbs. Add the zest and juice of one orange. Fill each veal escalope with the mixture and roll up and tie with string.

Melt the remaining butter and the oil in the frying pan and sauté the veal rolls until slightly browned. Stir in the coarsely grated orange rind and a pinch of thyme and cook on low heat for five minutes. Sprinkle as much Grand Marnier as you like over the veal. Shake the pan over the heat, add the orange juice, cornflour and water, season to taste and simmer for three minutes.

Cut each roll in half and arrange them on a serving dish and pour over the sauce. Decorate with bundles of fresh thyme and slices of orange.

White Chocolate Profiteroles and Dark Chocolate Sauce

Serves 12-14

Set oven at 200 C, 400 F, Gas Mark 6

125 g plain flour
100 g butter
300 ml water
4 small eggs, lightly beaten
Few drops vanilla essence
75 g icing sugar, sieved
25 g butter
568 ml double cream, whipped
150 g white chocolate Nestlé Milky Bar
6 tablespoons double cream

Chocolate sauce
150 g dark chocolate
3 tablespoons milk
25 g butter
75 ml weak black coffee

Sift flour on to a plate. Put butter and water together in a saucepan and heat gently until fat has melted, bring to boil. Remove pan from heat. Tip flour at once into liquid. Beat thoroughly with wooden spoon. Return to heat briefly and continue beating the mixture until smooth and glossy and it comes away from the side of the pan. Cool for two minutes and then gradually beat in the eggs until it reaches piping consistency. Pipe balls on to a non-stick damp baking tray and bake until golden and crispy. Do not open oven door until after ten minutes. Remove choux pastry from oven and pierce each ball to allow steam to escape and set to cool on a wire rack.

When profiteroles are cold, slit them and fill them with the whipped cream. Now carefully melt the white chocolate Nestlé Milky Bar over a very low heat with the six tablespoons of cream and the 25 g of butter. Add vanilla essence and icing sugar and beat until smooth. Allow the chocolate icing to become cold and thick and then spread over the profiteroles.

Now make the sauce. Melt the dark chocolate over a very low heat with the milk, butter and coffee stiring all the time until the sauce becomes smooth and glossy. Serve warm in a sauce boat. Pile the profiteroles on to a plate and keep chilled until needed.

Hot Gooseberry Sponge Pudding
Serves 8

There never seem to be any recipes for gooseberries and as we have so many at home, I made up this recipe which can be made with either fresh or frozen gooseberries.

Set oven at 180 C, 350 F, Gas Mark 4

> 1 kg gooseberries
> 100 g sugar
> 100 g butter
> 100 g caster sugar
> 2 eggs, beaten
> 225 g self-raising flour, sifted
> Pinch of salt
> 200 ml milk
> 1 teaspoon vanilla essence
> Caster sugar or icing sugar to dust

Cook the gooseberries in a little water with the 100 g sugar. Transfer them to a large deep ovenproof pie dish. Now make the sponge. Beat the butter and sugar together in a food processor. Gradually beat in the eggs. Mix the flour and salt and gradually incorporate them into the mixture with the milk and vanilla essence. Spoon the mixture over the gooseberries and bake for 45 minutes until the sponge is well risen and brown. Dust with caster sugar or icing sugar and serve hot with cream.

Banana and Rum Crumble

Serves 8

A wonderful, winter pudding that definitely sticks to the ribs!

Set oven at 190C, 375 F, Gas Mark 5

8 ripe bananas, peeled
3 tablespoons West Indian rum
425 ml fresh double cream
500 g Sainsbury's crumble mix
175 g crunchy oat cereal
Plenty of demerara sugar (according to taste)
A little butter

Slice the bananas in quarters and arrange in the bottom of a buttered oven-proof dish. Sprinkle with the rum and pour over the cream. Mix some of the sugar with the crumble mix and the crunchy oat cereal. Pat it firmly down on to the bananas and sprinkle with the remaining sugar. Bake for 30 minutes until browned and crunchy. Serve warm.

MENUS FOR RACE DAYS

Whether it is Royal Ascot week, York races or Cheltenham, race days are fun, usually cold, wet and muddy and occasionally boiling hot, dusty and always crowded, boozey and expensive!

Clever planning is needed for sucessful picnics. Make the list of everything you need, baskets, napkins, cutlery, clothes, glasses, salt and pepper and bottle openers and masses of other things. Double check everything the morning of the races to make sure nobody has lifted anything. If it is going to be Cheltenham you definately need a warming soup and buttered bread rolls followed by the following suggestions.

MENU FOR SIX

Watercress, spring onion and walnut Quiche
A cold potato salad of your choice
*   A good mixed salad (page 87) with walnut oil vinaigrette
     (page 81) (to be added last minute)
Lemon and pineapple roulade

Wine: *White Rhône, 1985 St. Joseph Blanc (throughout)*

Finish off with plentiful supplies of hot coffee, tea and milk. Don't forget a bag for all your rubbish and one for all the dirty plates etc.

For Ascot or any summer meeting I would be eternally optimistic and prepare food that will not go off or melt in the heat of the car boot.

MENU FOR SIX

Spinach roulade with smoked salmon and scrambled eggs
Chicken galantine with green peppercorns
Buttered bread rolls
Cold new potatoes
*   A good mixed salad (page 87) and walnut oil vinaigrette
     (page 81) (to be added at the last minute)
*   Grilled peppers in olive oil
*   Praline and strawberry tart

Wine: *Loire, 1989 Ménétou-Salon, Le Petit Clos, J.M. Roger*
               Red Bordeaux, 1985 Ch. Hervé-Laroque, Fronsac
               White Bordeaux, 1987, Ch. du Mont, Ste. Croix du Mont

I suggest making two tarts because you are bound to collect a few extra mouths to feed by that time!

Watercress, Spring Onion and Walnut Quiche
Serves 6

This is a delightful and cheap quiche to make for a party or a picnic and makes a change from the more traditional recipes.

Set oven at 190 C, 375 F, Gas Mark 5

> 454 g packet shortcrust pastry
> 2 bunches spring onions, trimmed
> 50 g butter
> 2 bunches watercress, trimmed
> 4 eggs
> 4 heaped tablespoons Greek strained yoghurt
> Salt, pepper and nutmeg
> 100 g grated cheese
> 50 g chopped walnuts
> Cayenne pepper

Roll out the shortcrust pastry, and line a greased and floured quiche dish. Cook the onions in the butter until soft. Stir in the watercress and walnuts. Beat the eggs, Greek yoghurt and seasoning in a bowl and stir in the hot onions and watercress. Quickly pour into the pastry case. Sprinkle over the grated cheese and cayenne pepper and bake for 25 minutes until just firm and golden.

Lemon and Pineapple Roulade

Serves 6

Set oven at 190 C, 375 F, Gas Mark 5

4 large eggs, separated
100 g caster sugar
Zest of 1 small lemon
Juice of 1 $1/2$ lemons
40 g plain flour
Pinch of salt
284 ml double cream, whipped
$1/2$ fresh pineapple, chopped
Caster sugar
Bakewell paper

Line a swiss roll tin with Bakewell paper and secure. Combine the egg yolks with the sugar in the Magimix with the zest and juice of the lemons. Beat until pale and fluffy. Mix the flour and salt and sift into the lemon mixture. Beat the egg whites until stiff and fold into the lemon mixture. Spoon into the prepared tin and bake for 20 minutes or until firm to touch. Cover with a damp cloth until a little cooler and then turn out the roulade on to another piece of Bakewell paper with sifted caster sugar on it.

Roll up the roulade and chill. Carefully unroll the roulade and spread one third of the cream with most of the chopped pineapple over the inside of the roulade and roll it up. Now pipe flat swirls of cream all over the top of the roulade and decorate with a few pieces of pineapple. Chop up the remaining half of the pineapple and use the leaves, if they are in good condition, as decoration around the roulade.

Spinach Roulade with Smoked Salmon and Scrambled Eggs

Serves 6 - 8

This roulade is very good, either hot in winter or cold in summer which is when I tasted it, lapping up the Norfolk sunshine and enjoying Panda Allhusen's delicious food.

Set oven at 200 C, 400 F, Gas Mark 6

Bakewell paper	*Filling*
450 g cooked, drained, finely chopped spinach	100 g smoked salmon
4 large eggs	4 large eggs
12 g butter	100 ml single cream
Salt, pepper and nutmeg	Salt and pepper
Grated Parmesan cheese	12 g butter
	Parsley, salmon twists or quails eggs to decorate

First line a Swiss roll tin with Bakewell paper. Cook the spinach for a few minutes to make sure all the water is gone. Remove from the heat and stir in the egg yolks, butter, salt, pepper and nutmeg. In a bowl beat the egg whites until stiff and fold into the spinach. Carefully pour the mixture into the tin, sprinkle with Parmesan cheese and bake for 10-15 minutes until firm to touch.

Cut the salmon into little pieces. Beat the eggs, cream, salt and pepper together in a bowl. Gently scramble the eggs in the butter - they should be slightly runny. Cool briefly while you turn out the roulade on to a piece of greaseproof paper, sprinkled with Parmesan cheese. Mix the salmon with the eggs and spread this mixture on to the roulade, roll up and serve immediately or chill. Use your imagination to decorate the length of the roulade with little sprigs of parsley, salmon twists and perhaps halved quails eggs.

Chicken Galantine with Green Peppercorns

Serves 6

Set oven at 190 C, 375 F, Gas Mark 5

> 1.8 kg boned weight, fresh chicken
> 100 g prosciutto, thinly sliced
> 350 g lean minced pork
> 225 ml double cream
> Salt, pepper and nutmeg
> 1 tablespoon green peppercorns
> Olive oil
> Watercress to decorate

Bone the chicken with a very sharp knife. Spread the chicken on a board, skin side down and cover with the prosciutto. Mix the pork, cream, seasoning, peppercorns and any remaining chicken pieces, in a bowl. Spread this mixture on to the prosciutto and roll up the chicken like a sausage, brushing the skin with oil, wrapping in some foil and then chill for 30 minutes.

Roast the chicken for about one hour or until the juices run clear. When you remove the chicken from the oven, keep it in the foil for 20 minutes before unwrapping it and carving. Serve the chicken in its own jelly decorated with watercress.

Grilled Peppers in Olive Oil

Serves 6

I used to prepare these peppers when I was living in New York as they are so easy and colourful - ideal for the hot humid summer. They are even better the next day.

2 red peppers
2 yellow peppers
2 green peppers
$^1/_2$ cup virgin olive oil
2 cloves garlic, crushed
Fresh or dried thyme
Black pepper

Cut the peppers in half and remove the seeds and trim the ends. Mix the oil, garlic and thyme together in a cup and brush each pepper skin with the mixture. Grill the peppers until the skins start to blister and burn. Take a very sharp knife and peel off the skin and slice the peppers into strips. Leave to marinate in the remaining oil and chill until needed.

Serve with freshly ground black pepper and warm fresh bread.

Praline and Strawberry Tart
Serves 10

I made this once with such a hangover that I used a plastic spatula to stir the praline and I didn't even notice that it was getting shorter and shorter until I washed up what was left! My clients said the pudding was delicious but a little bit chewy!

2 Sainsbury's sweet shortcrust pastry cases
100 g whole blanched almonds
100 g caster sugar
284 ml double cream
500 g ripe strawberries, hulled
300 g redcurrant jelly

Melt the sugar and almonds over medium heat until they begin to caramelize. Shake a little and continue to cook until quite brown. Turn on to greased non-stick paper to set.

Whip the cream. Melt the jelly, halve the strawberries and then grind the cold praline in the Magimix. Fold this into the cream and spoon over the base of each flan. Cover with the strawberries and glaze with the jelly. Chill before serving.

MENUS FOR LAZY SUMMER OR WINTER WEEKENDS FOR EIGHT

My idea of bliss is to have a really lazy weekend in the country. However as the hostess this is seldom achieved without rallying around the guests and persuading them it is fun to chop up logs, wash up and lay the table! So, here are some very easy menus for Saturday night supper parties in the kitchen, or out in the garden in the summer. My main advice for the weekend is not to overload yourself with things to do, so do all the shopping on Thursday or Friday. If you are already in the country at this stage, make the soup and ice cream. If not make them first thing Saturday morning after breakfast. The fish can be cooked on a BBQ and the potatoes and salad prepared at the last minute.

For the second menu you can cook the pheasant and make the pudding the day before your guests arrive so you have plenty of time to spend with them. You should start to do everything else an hour before dinner.

SUMMER MENU FOR EIGHT

	Chilled prawn, pea and mint soup
*	Spiked grilled Swordfish
*	A continental salad, (page 81)
	New potatoes
*	Greek lemon ice cream

Wine: *Sherry, Manzanilla*
          White Rioja, 1988 Marqués de Cáceres, Seco
          Loire, 1983 Coteaux du Layon, Vignoble du Sauveroy

Counting Sheep

WINTER MENU FOR EIGHT

       Warm chicken liver and oyster mushroom salad
*   Pheasant Indiana
*   Wild rice (page 51)
*   Aromatic carrots with cloves (page 52)
*   Chocolate biscuit cake (page 65)
*   Crème chantilly (page 61)

Wine: *Red Loire, 1988 Chinon, Domaine du Roncée*
           Red Burgundy, 1985 Côtes de Nuits Villages, Lupé-Cholet
           Eau de Vie, Framboise, E. Boekel

Make life easy for yourself in the summer, give everybody lovely fresh fruit and croissants for Saturday breakfast and free-range boiled eggs and toast on Sunday. Most people are so health and figure conscious anyway that they do not want a huge cooked breakfast. Keep lunch very light if you can't go to a nice pub. In summer I let everybody BBQ sausages and have a huge continental salad and a selection of cheeses and fruit.

In winter I usually buy or make a filling soup or pâté, served with french bread and a good selection of cheeses and fruit.

Afternoon tea is definitely off and Sunday lunch is simply something like this;

Summer	Winter
* Italian roast pork	* Traditional roast lamb
Fresh pasta and Parmesan	Roquefort and rosemary gratin
cheese	of potatoes
* A good mixed salad (page 87)	Broccoli
* Italian baked peaches	Apple frangipane tart
Fresh cream	Fresh cream

Wine: Italy. 1986 Castello di Nipozzano, *Wine: Chile, 1986 Dom Maximiano,*
      Chianti Rúfina Riserva   *Cabernet Sauvignon*
      Hock, 1985 Oppenheimer   *Moselle, 1988 Piesporter*
        Sackträger, Riesling Auslese,   *Goldtropfchen, Riesling Auslese,*
        Weingut Louis Guntrum   *Reichsgraf von Kesselstatt*

Chilled Prawn, Pea and Mint Soup

Serves 8

If you are making the soup in advance, leave out the prawns until an hour before serving.

>1 large onion, peeled and finely sliced
>750 g frozen peas
>100 g butter
>Salt, pepper and nutmeg
>1 stock cube, made up to 600 ml stock
>300 ml milk
>600 ml cream
>1 bunch fresh mint leaves
>$^1/_2$ tablespoon caster sugar
>225 g fresh prawns

Cook the onion in butter until soft, season with salt, pepper, nutmeg and sugar and add the stock, peas and mint. Simmer for 20 minutes. Cool the soup and liquidize with the milk and transfer to a bowl. Stir in the cream and prawns and chill until needed.

Spiked Grilled Swordfish

Serves 8

This is great on a BBQ or grilled. Ideal for the summer an idea which a wonderful American friend of mine, Jeannie, gave to me in New York.

>8 swordfish steaks
>4 tablespoons soy sauce
>4 tablespoons sesame oil
>4 tablespoons runny honey
>1 tablespoon ground ginger
>Salt and pepper

Mix all the ingredients together and marinate the swordfish for a few hours. BBQ or grill the fish under or over very high heat basting from time to time with the marinade. Serve hot with salads.

Warm Chicken Liver and Oyster Mushroom Salad

Serves 4

This recipe doubles up nicely to serve eight people.

> 40 g lambs lettuce
> 100 g packet frisée and radicchio salad mix
> 2 tablespoons olive oil
> 100 g small shallots, peeled
> 1 tablespoon caster sugar
> 150 g oyster mushrooms, in small pieces
> 50 g butter
> 1 teaspoon coriander seeds
> Salt and pepper
> 227 g chicken livers
> 3 tablespoons Balsamic vinegar

Fry the shallots over medium heat in the oil until brown all over and soft through the centre. Add the tablespoon of caster sugar to coat the shallots and leave to glaze for five minutes. In another frying pan sauté the mushrooms cut into manageable pieces in 50 g butter with salt, pepper and coriander seeds.

Now rinse the chicken livers in a sieve and leave to drain. Pat dry with kitchen towel and chop into small pieces and add to the mushrooms and brown them quickly. Stir in the Balsamic vinegar and shake the pan vigorously, add the shallots and mix together. Neatly arrange the salads on to four plates and spoon the sauté of livers and mushrooms on to the salads pouring over all the juices left in the pan. Serve immediately.

Greek Lemon Ice Cream

Serves 8 - 12

Instant success in the summer, this is a completely foolproof, no cooking ice cream which hardly needs any stirring either.

> 2 x 450 g Greek strained yoghurt
> 300 ml double cream
> 225 g caster sugar
> Juice of 5 lemons
> Grated zest of ¹/₂ lemon

Put the Greek yoghurt into a mixing bowl and add the sugar and cream. Add the lemon juice and zest and mix together. Freeze in a container.

After a few hours, mix and turn the ice cream with a fork, and return to the freezer until needed. Soften the ice cream a little before serving with biscuits or petits fours.

© 1991 Kellogg Company

Pheasant Indiana

Serves 8

This sauce is marvellous because it is perfect over chicken and I often use it for hot buffets and I can't thank Jane Sayer enough for giving it to me at a dinner party last year.

Set oven at 190 C, 375 F, Gas Mark 5

>3 cooked pheasants carved into slices and legs skinned
>500 ml double cream
>4 tablespoons Lea and Perrins Worcestershire sauce
>4 tablespoons Sharwood Mango Chutney
>Salt and pepper

Arrange the pheasant in a deep ovenproof dish or casserole. As the cream melts it will overflow if the dish is too shallow. In a big mixing bowl whip the cream until firm peaks hold, then stir in the Lea and Perrins, chutney and seasoning. Spoon the sauce over the pheasant and bake for 20 minutes until browned and bubbling.

Italian Roast Pork

Serves 8

An aromatic Tuscan way of cooking meat dating back to the 17th century. This is delicious hot or cold with hot pasta.

Set oven at 190 C, 375 F, Gas Mark 5

> 1.6 kg loin of pork, skinned, boned and tied
> 12 sage leaves
> 8 cloves
> 4 cloves garlic, halved
> Salt and pepper
> Grated zest of 2 lemons
> 300 ml white wine
> 1 glass of water

Rub the meat with salt and pepper and insert the cloves and the garlic into the meat. Tuck the sage leaves into the strings. Cover with lemon zest. Put into a roasting tin with the wine and marinate for 12 hours.

Roast the pork for one and a half hours or cook until the juices run clear. Baste occasionally, adding more white wine and a glass of water if necessary.

Serve the pork with noodles tossed in the pork juices, extra butter and grated Parmesan.

Italian Baked Peaches

Serves 8 - 10

Set oven at 180 C, 375 F, Gas Mark 5

4 or 5 large ripe peaches
80 g Amaretti biscuits
2-3 tablespoons Cointreau
6 tablespoons sugar
1 egg yolk
8-10 blanched almonds
25 g butter
150 ml white wine

Crush the amaretti with the end of a rolling pin in a small bowl. Rinse and dry the peaches, cut in half and remove the stones. Scoop out a little extra flesh with a teaspoon and add it to the amaretti, Cointreau, sugar and egg yolk. Spoon the filling into each peach and place an almond on top of each one. Place them in a buttered ovenproof dish and pour over the wine.

Bake until lightly browned but don't let the peaches split.

Serve with crème chantilly (page 61).

Roquefort and Rosemary Gratin of Potatoes
Serves 8

This is delicious with any plain roast or with steak and I'm afraid I can eat all of it without any meat at all!

Set oven at 200 C, 400 F, Gas Mark 6

> 2 kg old potatoes, peeled and finely sliced
> 175 g butter
> Salt and pepper
> 125 g Roquefort cheese
> Fresh rosemary
> 600 ml milk
> 150 ml double cream

Butter a large gratin dish and cover with layers of potato, butter, salt, pepper, milk, small cubes of cheese and rosemary until they are all used up. Leave just enough butter to dot over the top. Finally pour the cream over the top with a sprinkling of salt and pepper and bake for one hour and 30 minutes in the oven until soft inside and browned on top.

Apple Frangipane Tart
Serves 8

Set oven at 190 C, 375 F, Gas Mark 5

500 g packet fresh shortcrust pastry
285 g jar Sainsbury's apple sauce
725 g eating apples
Juice of one lemon
50 g butter
50 g caster sugar
125 g ground almonds
1 teaspoon almond essence

1 tablespoon Langdales' Essence of Rose
  water
1 egg yolk
50 g self raising flour
1 level teaspoon baking powder
2 tablespoon milk
2 egg whites
50 g flaked almonds

Grease and flour a large fluted flan dish. Roll out the pastry on a floured surface and line dish. Trim edges and prick all over the base with a fork. Keep chilled while you continue preparing the recipe.

Now peel and core the apples and slice very finely into a bowl of lemon juice and toss evenly. Spoon the apple sauce into the chilled pastry case and layer the sliced apples over the sauce.

In a food processor cream the butter and sugar together and beat in the ground almonds, essences and the egg yolk. Sift the flour and baking powder into the processor bowl then mix quickly, adding the milk.

In a separate bowl whisk the two egg whites until stiff and then fold the creamed mixture into the egg whites. Spread this over the apples, scatter with flaked almonds and bake for 45 minutes or until the apples are soft and the top is golden. If the top gets too brown, cover with foil until the apples are fully cooked this will prevent the almonds from burning. Serve warm with cream or crème chantilly (page 61).

COPING WITH CHRISTMAS
AND MENUS

The build up to Christmas is far too long, totally hyped up and we are led to believe that we must spend a fortune on presents, decorations, food and drink, all in the name of Christmas spirit. I must admit a week before I do get excited and rush off to buy a holly wreath but I never quite have the nerve to put it on the front door because I know it will get pinched! So I ended up using it as a centre piece for my dining room table and smartened it up with little gold baubles and miniature Christmas presents. I then put the candlestick in the centre and it looked great. I even extended the dining room table and put a wreath at each end which looked very effective. For the centre piece I found a china fruit stand, covered it with evergreen from the garden and piled it high with bright red apples which I had polished. The same colour red candles and napkins started to bring it all together. Some wonderful miniature wreaths with tiny fir-cones caught my eye so I bought those and put them in front of every guest with their place card set in them. We had a huge Christmas tree covered in candles and tartan ribbons and a few gold baubles and piles of presents spilling out over the floor. With the lights off and the fire roaring the scene was set for a marvellous Christmas Eve.

All this time however I was busy making lists and lists of things to get me through Christmas. You cannot afford to forget anything with the shops closing for three days. This obviously all depends on how many people you are feeding over Christmas or New Year as to how much you need to do in advance. I can highly recommend doing absolutely everything possible, otherwise you will never leave the kitchen.

A fairly safe hit list is to plan your days menu by menu, even breakfast and tea for the children etc. That ensures nothing is overlooked. Do all the non-perishable shopping a week or two in advance and store it away from sticky fingers. Put as much as possible in the deep freeze, all the bacon, sausages, bread, butter, mincepies and ice cream. Brussel sprouts and cranberries can also be frozen. This avoids last minute panic shopping when you have to stand in a queue for an hour to buy eight things! It helps to write a list of everything you have made or bought and put in the deep freeze. I have just prepared menus for Christmas Eve and Boxing Day as I believe in cooking the traditional Christmas Day lunch or dinner and Delia Smith has a brilliant 'Count Down to Christmas Lunch' in one of her cook books.

Another relaxing Christmas

Menu for Christmas Eve
Serves 6

*   Quails eggs and prawn salad
*   Roast wood pigeon with wild rowan jelly sauce
    Courgettes with onions and cream
    Frozen or fresh croquette potatoes
     (Marks and Spencer have the best)
    Mincemeat in filo parcels and brandy sauce
    Stilton, oatcakes, Port and coffee

In the early evening or late afternoon get your cheese and biscuits laid out, decant the Port and set the coffee tray. Then make the pudding up to the cooking stage and the sauce and set aside. Prepare all the ingredients for the salad ready to put together. Get the pigeon into the oven and cook the vegetables, keeping them warm while you make the sauce for the pigeon. Assemble the salads and place them on to the table. As you sit down put the pudding in the oven to be taken out while you are clearing away the plates. Heat through the sauce just before serving the starter.

Wine: *White Bordeaux, 1987 Ch. Bouscaut, Graves*
        Red Burgundy, 1983 Le Corton, Doudet-Naudin
        White Bordeaux, 1986 Ch. Liot, Barsac
        Berrys' Own Selection Vintage Character Port

Quails Eggs and Prawn Salad
Serves 6

This is an ideal starter for a dinner party if you are short of time. A good piece of advice is to boil the eggs for two minutes so that they do not go rubbery and peel the eggs a day in advance, tie them up in a plastic bag and chill until needed.

12 quails eggs
1 bunch asparagus
227 g Sainsbury's extra large peeled prawns, fresh or frozen
200 g packet continental salad mix of frisée and radicchio
100 g packet edible nasturtium flowers or
15 g packet of fresh basil leaves

Dill Sauce
$^3/_4$ tablespoon dill weed
3 tablespoons Total Greek strained yoghurt
Fresh black pepper and salt
Walnut oil vinaigrette (page 81)

Hard boil the eggs and peel them under cold water. Trim the asparagus and cook in boiling salted water until tender. Drain and rinse under cold water and lay them on some absorbent paper. Peel the fresh prawns leaving the tails on and rinse them or thaw the frozen prawns. Arrange the salad on six plates, cut the asparagus in half, using just the tips, and place with the prawns on the salad. Cut the eggs in half and add to the salad with a scattering of flowers or basil leaves.

Make the sauce. In a bowl mix the vinaigrette with the dill and Greek yoghurt, and season to taste. Mix until smooth and creamy. Trickle the sauce over the salad and serve with french bread or warm rolls.

Roast Wood Pigeon
with Wild Rowan Jelly Sauce
Serves 6

A marvellous tip for any roast game is to serve it with redcurrant or rowan jelly mixed with a little Worcestershire sauce, so here is a recipe on that theme.

Set oven at 200 C, 400 F, or Gas Mark 6

> 6 wood pigeon
> 6 knobs of butter
> 6 shallots peeled and chopped
> Fresh thyme
> Salt and black pepper
> 225 g rindless streaky bacon
> 300 ml red wine
> 2 tablespoons olive oil
> 175 g Baxter's Wild Rowan Jelly
> 3 teaspoons Worcestershire sauce

Clean and dry the wood pigeon and place in a roasting tin. Cover with the streaky bacon and sprinkle with thyme, salt and pepper. Place a knob of butter on each one. Finely chop the shallots and scatter around the birds. Sprinkle the oil over the shallots and roast in the oven for 20 minutes.

Remove birds from oven and baste and add red wine. Return to oven for a further 15 minutes. Arrange a bird on each plate or alternatively carve the breast and arrange in a fan shape on each plate.

Drain off any excess fat, put the pan on the hob and boil up with the jelly and Worcestershire sauce. When the sauce is smooth and well blended, sieve into a jug and spoon over the carved breasts or serve the sauce separately with the whole birds.

Courgettes with Onions and Cream
Serves 6

These courgettes are delicious with roast or grilled meat and are ideal for dinner parties if you don't want to spend a lot of time making a sauce for the meat.

> 500 g courgettes, topped and tailed
> 2 small onions, sliced into very fine rings
> 50 g butter
> Salt and pepper
> Rosemary and nutmeg
> 150 ml double cream

Blanch the courgettes in boiling water, drain and refresh under cold water. Now cook the onions until soft but not brown in the butter preferably in a non-stick frying pan. Stir in the seasoning, rosemary and nutmeg to your taste, add the courgettes and lastly the cream and simmer for five to ten minutes until the sauce is thick.

Serve with roast chicken, veal or lamb.

Mincemeat in Filo Parcels
and Brandy Sauce
Serves 6

This is a great alternative to mince pies and brandy butter and is also ideal for using up your leftover mincemeat in the New Year.

Set oven at 200 C, 400 F, Gas Mark 6

> 6 heaped tablespoons mincemeat
> Juice of $1/2$ lemon
> 12 leaves of filo pastry, unfrozen
> 175 g butter
> Ground cinnamon
> Caster sugar

Mix the mincemeat and lemon juice together. Melt the butter in a saucepan. Place two leaves of pastry on top of each other and brush with melted butter. Spoon on the mincemeat and wrap up into a parcel. Brush with more butter, sprinkle with cinnamon and sugar and place on a non-stick baking tray. Repeat this until you have made the six parcels. Bake in the oven for ten minutes and then brush with more butter, return to the oven and bake for another ten minutes until crispy. Serve immediately glazed with more butter if there is any left and accompany with the brandy sauce.

> *Brandy Sauce*
> 4 egg yolks
> 100 g caster sugar
> 3 tablespoons freshly squeezed orange juice
> Grated zest of 1 orange
> 3 tablespoons brandy
> 300 ml double cream

Whisk the egg yolks, sugar and zest in a food processor gradually add the orange juice, brandy and cream. Stir the custard over very low heat in a non-stick saucepan until thick. Do not boil. Whisk continuously for a minute or two when removed from the heat. Then pour into a sauceboat and serve.

Boxing Day Lunch
Serves 8 - 12

By this time everyone is well and truly fed up with mincepies etc. so here is something slightly different for your guests.

MENU

Cranberry and orange stuffed pork en croûte
Spiced red cabbage and apple (page 93)
*   Creamed potatoes (page 42)
*   Ginger and brandysnap ice cream with butterscotch sauce
Clementines, nuts, fresh lychees and coffee

The delight of this menu is that you can made the ice cream days in advance and keep the butterscotch sauce in a sealed jar for a few days and heat it up just before serving. You can also freeze the red cabbage and heat it through from room temperature and have the potatoes peeled in water ready to cook and mash. You can organise all this while the pork en croûte is cooking.

Wine: *Rhône, 1983 Hermitage Rouge*
           The King's Ginger Liqueur

Cranberry and Orange Stuffed Pork en Croûte

Serves 8 - 12

The joy of a recipe like this is that not only is it so quick but it is easy to carve because it is boneless.

Set oven at 190 C, 375 F, Mark 5

> 1.7 kg loin of pork (boned and skinned weight)
> 2 x 80 g packets Knorr cider apple herb stuffing
> 1 egg
> 2 x 265 g jars Sainsbury's luxury cranberry sauce with Port
> Salt and pepper
> 300 g frozen Jus-rol filo pastry
> Oil
> A couple of tablespoons of Port

Empty the packets of stuffing into a bowl and add six tablespoons of boiling water and the egg with one pot of cranberry sauce. Spoon the stuffing along the inside of the pork and fold over. Season the meat and then wrap up in filo pastry. Brush with oil and bake in the oven for one hour and 15 minutes. You must keep foil loosely over it to protect the pastry. Lift this off 15 minutes before the end of cooking time to brown and crispen the pastry. You should baste the pork en croûte occasionally with more oil during cooking time.

Carve the meat and serve the remaining cranberry sauce mixed with a couple of tablespoons of Port in a sauceboat.

Ginger and Brandysnap Ice Cream with Butterscotch Sauce

Serves 12

All my friends vote this ice cream their absolute favourite and I have to say that I totally agree with them, it's quite wicked with the butterscotch sauce.

454 g ginger preserve
340 g stem ginger in syrup
2 x 100 g packets brandysnaps
1 litre double cream
Mint leaves for decoration

Butterscotch Sauce
100 g butter
100 g demerara sugar
225 g golden syrup
150 ml single cream

Keep quarter of the stem ginger to use as decoration.

Mix the preserve and syrup together and finely chop three quarters of the stem ginger and mix them all together. Break up all the brandysnaps into small pieces. In another big bowl whip up all the cream until it reaches soft peak stage and then carefully fold in the preserve and the brandysnaps and freeze for three to four hours. Stir once to keep it soft and then seal and refreeze.

To make the butterscotch sauce, put the first three ingredients in a saucepan and melt until dissolved then bring to the boil for three minutes. Remove from heat and allow bubbles to subside. Gradually stir in the cream and heat until smooth.

To serve, place a huge scoop of ice cream on each plate and decorate the edge of the plates with slithers of stem ginger and little mint leaves and serve the sauce separately. As a final touch, add a plate of Askeys fan wafers.

MENUS FOR NEW YEAR

There are so many different ways of spending New Year, it is hard to decide whether I should do menus for a weekend with friends or a family gathering. As I always organise a party to take a house in Cornwall, Gloucestershire or Shropshire, I have put down a couple of menus which need little work. Both menus can be doubled up to make enough for parties of twelve. If you are working all day and can only get home in the early evening to do your New Year's Eve party, then the menus would suit you very well enabling you to enjoy yourself and not be stuck in the kitchen all night.

New Year's Eve Party

MENU FOR TWELVE

* Smoked duck and pawpaw in garlic and rosemary vinaigrette
* Fillet steaks in Cassis and pink peppercorn sauce
  Chocolate and coffee bean gâteau (page 26)
* Cheating raspberry crème brûlée

An extravagant menu for New Year. A new beginning, old friends and a special treat for everybody. Keep the portions small to keep costs down, everyone is still so full from Christmas they will be perfectly happy, especially if they are knocking back the bubbly.

You can make both the puddings a day in advance and grill the crèmes brûlées in the early evening and return them to the fridge until needed. Prepare the salad next and plate up and set on the table with bread rolls and butter. Then you can forget about it until you light the candles for dinner. Put all the ingredients and pans ready by your hob so that you can cook the steaks before everyone arrives. Make sure they are very rare. You can then leave them until you have finished your starter when you can sauté the steaks in the sauce for a few minutes while someone else clears the plates away for you.

Wine: *Beaujolais 1989, Moulin-à-Vent, Thorin*
             New Zealand, 1987 Babich Irongate Cabernet / Merlot
             Eau de Vie, Framboise, E. Boekel

Smoked Duck and Pawpaw in Garlic and Rosemary Vinaigrette
Serves 6

This doubles up nicely for a dinner party for twelve and has the advantage of not needing any cooking at all.

A large bunch of lambs lettuce
100 g packet frisée and radicchio salad mix
1 ripe pawpaw, seeds removed
Two smoked duck breasts, skins removed
1 clove crushed garlic
Fresh rosemary
150 ml walnut oil vinaigrette (page 81)

Quarter the pawpaw and cut into slices. Carve the duck breasts into slices and make the vinaigrette adding to the basic recipe some crushed garlic and fresh rosemary.

Divide the salad and lambs lettuce on to six plates and arrange the slices of pawpaw and smoked duck on top. Sprinkle with the dressing and serve.

A Dis-jointed Duck

Fillet steaks in Cassis and Pink Peppercorn Sauce

Serves 12

A firm favourite with the men, I often cook this for the numerous stag nights I get asked to cater for in London. Not a recipe for anyone on a tight budget.

12 fillet steaks
4 shallots, peeled and finely chopped
1 bay-leaf
Salt and pepper
Pinch of fresh thyme
2 tablespoons redcurrant jelly
2 tablespoons pink peppercorns, drained
1 tablespoon butter
2 tablespoons Cognac
2 tablespoons Crème de Cassis
4 tablespoons olive oil

Cook the shallots in two tablespoons of oil in a large frying pan until soft but not brown. Add the bay-leaf, salt, pepper and branch or pinch of thyme. Sauté the steaks in another frying pan in two tablespoons of oil, four at a time until all twelve are cooked but rare. Transfer eight of the steaks to a serving dish and keep warm. Transfer the remaining steaks and juices from that pan into the pan with the shallots.

As soon as you think your guests are nearly ready turn the hob up very high, pour the Cognac over the steaks, shake vigorously and repeat with the Cassis. Blend the jelly and peppercorns and stir. Remove the bay-leaf. Transfer the steaks to warm plates. Add the remaining steaks to the sauce to briefly heat through. Stir the butter into the sauce to make it thick and glossy and spoon immediately over all the steaks and serve.

Cheating Raspberry Crème Brûlée
Serves 8

This recipe avoids cooking the crème brûlée in an oven and hence is easier and quicker. It can also be made a day in advance and brûléed half an hour before being eaten. You can use ramekins or a soufflé dish.

> 600 ml double cream
> Vanilla essence
> 4 egg yolks
> 100 g caster sugar
> 11 g sachet gelatine
> 200 g fresh raspberries, cleaned and hulled

Heat the cream gently until boiling, add plenty of vanilla essence and remove from the heat. Beat the egg yolks and 50 g of the sugar together in the Magimix until light and creamy. Gradually pour in the hot cream beating all the time. Dissolve the gelatine as instructed on the packet. Return the custard to the saucepan and cook gently over lowish heat until the custard is thick. Do not boil the custard. Remove from the heat and stir constantly for five minutes and then stir in the gelatine. Leave to cool, stirring occasionally. Place a few raspberries in the bottom of each ramekin or put them in the soufflé dish and pour the custard over them. Cover with clingfilm and chill for as long as possible. Sprinkle the remaining sugar over the top of the chilled creams and caramelise under a pre-heated hot grill for a couple of seconds. Chill before serving.

New Year's Day Lunch

MENU FOR SIX

*   Chinese roast pork
*   Quick cauliflower au gratin
*   Sesame seed roast potatoes (page 24)
     Rhubarb and orange mousse
     Chocolates, nuts and coffee

Marinate the pork first, then make the pudding, decorate and chill. Next do the roast potatoes and the cauliflower. Now get the meat in the oven and during the last hour heat through the cauliflower and make the sauce.

Chinese Roast Pork
Serves 6

Set oven at 190 C, 375 F, Gas Mark 5

1.1 kg - 1.5 kg boneless leg of pork with skin
100 ml sunflower oil
100 ml dry white wine
100 ml cider vinegar
125 ml orange juice
1 $^1/_2$ teaspoons Old El Paso hot taco sauce
1 $^1/_2$ dessertspoons Rajah Lime Pickle
3 tablespoons double concentrate tomato purée
Salt and freshly milled pepper
2 heaped tablespoons of dark muscovado sugar

Put all the ingredients in a bowl and mix together. Pour into a medium sized non-stick roasting tin leaving just enough to spread over the top of the pork when it is in the pan. Leave to marinate for 30 minutes on each side at room temperature.

Roast in the oven for about two hours until the pork is brown and crispy and the juices run clear from inside. Take the meat out of the pan and leave for five minutes and then carve on to a warm plate. Now carefully pour any fat lying on top of the sauce away. Scrape around the pan with a wooden spoon, add a couple of tablespoons of water and stir over medium heat until bubbling. Pour the sauce over the pork and serve.

Quick Cauliflower au Gratin

Serves 6

On the basis that I hate making any sort of white or cheese sauce, here is a short cut that never fails!

Set oven at 190C, 375 F, Gas Mark 5

1 large cauliflower, trimmed
450 g Greek strained yoghurt
Salt and pepper
4 tablespoons of cream
75 g Parmesan cheese, grated
Pinch of cayenne pepper
50 g butter, in small pieces

Cut the cauliflower into florets and cook in boiling, salted water until al dente. Drain and refresh under cold water. Transfer to a greased oven proof gratin dish.

In a small bowl mix the yoghurt with plenty of salt, pepper and the cream. Spoon this mixture on to the cauliflower and sprinkle with the grated Parmesan, then the cayenne pepper and lastly dot with butter. You can either refrigerate until needed or cook straight away until gold and bubbly.

Rhubarb and Orange Mousse
Serves 6 - 8

The rhubarb is heavily disguised so that even those who profess to hate rhubarb will love this pudding.

900 g rhubarb
Plenty of sugar
1 very large orange, juice, pulp and zest
300 ml cream, whipped
11 g powdered gelatine
50 g caster sugar
1 tablespoon Grand Marnier
1 orange cut into segments for decoration

Before you start put the orange juice, pulp and zest in a bowl together with the sugar and Grand Marnier and chill for as long as possible. Dissolve the gelatine according to the instructions.

Cook the rhubarb with plenty of sugar and a tiny bit of water until soft. Drain for a few seconds and transfer to a big bowl. Stir the gelatine into the rhubarb, now stir in the orange mixture and chill until the mixture begins to thicken. Fold in the cream and transfer to a pretty bowl. Decorate with segments of orange and chill until needed.

PLANNING FOR EASTER

For those of us who gave up chocolate for Lent this is D Day. Sometimes I wonder if I should start up Chocoholics Anonymous for those of us with absolutely no will power at all.

To plan for an Easter weekend at home I do all the menus first and then a massive shopping list including Easter eggs. My favourite Easter eggs which I provide every year are from Thorntons who write the child's or friend's name in white on each egg for you. This is a marvellous idea for Easter egg hunts and guarantees that each child gets an egg for her or himself. I usually hide a couple of dozen Cadbury's Creme Eggs as well to make the hunt last longer. At this point, having got them all outside, a well organised treasure hunt gets every-body out of the way and amused for a few hours on a Sunday afternoon. On the theme of eggs, Good Friday wouldn't be the same without boiled eggs and hot cross buns for breakfast. I personally share the Catholic view that it should be a sober day of light food and not too much to drink.

I suggest you get the children to hand paint their Easter Sunday breakfast hard boiled eggs on the Saturday and why not have something light and different like fruit salad and croissants so that you have room for a huge lunch.

Good Friday Menu

LUNCH FOR SIX

       Basil and gruyère soufflé
*   Sardines Napolitana
*   A good mixed salad (page 87)
*   Wild Rice (page 51)
       Fruit, cheese and coffee

Wine: *Italy, 1988 Castello di Cacchiano,*
            Chianti Classico (throughout)

A soufflé for lunch with a salad and fresh fish is an ideal quick lunch followed by the fruit, cheese and coffee which can all be prepared an hour before lunch. Then for dinner, if you are going to church beforehand you can make the pancakes and freeze them to reheat when you get back or make them in the morning and reheat them once the baked potatoes and the vegetables are cooked. The strawberry pudding can be made that morning too.

DINNER FOR EIGHT

Courgette and dill soup (page 127)
Haddock, tomato and asparagus pancakes
Baked potatoes, salad and green beans or peas and fresh mint
*   Strawberry and Amaretti whip

Wine: *Sherry, Almacenista, Manzanilla Pasada de Sanlúcar,*
        Manuel Cuevas Jurado
        California, Wente Bros. Chardonnay, Central Coast
        Moselle, 1988 Traben-Trarbacher Kräuterhaus, Riesling
        Auslese, C.A. Haussmann Erben

Easter Sunday

If you are a large party of twelve, double up on the rack of lamb recipe or cook two legs instead. Double up on the vegetables. The profiteroles are ample for twelve guests.

Rack of lamb in ginger, honey and herb glaze (page 74)
Celeriac purée (page 25)
*   Sesame seed roast potatoes (page 24)
*   Aromatic carrots with cloves (page 52)
*   White chocolate profiteroles and dark chocolate sauce (page 135)

Wine: *Red Bordeaux, 1985 Ch. Plagnac, Médoc*
        Fine Old Bas Armagnac

If you would rather cook traditional plain roast lamb which I love, serve it with fresh mint sauce, it is so easy to make. Snip up fresh mint and mix it with caster sugar and vinegar until it tastes sweet and tangy.

I try to keep off chocolate puddings as the children will be launching themselves into Easter eggs as soon as lunch is over, but as always the temptation overcomes my better judgement!

I love decorating the dining room table and Easter is a wonderful opportunity to use your imagination. Lots of daffodils and blossoms around the room but on the table I love baskets of hand painted eggs or Suchard's miniature chocolate eggs mixed with twigs and blossoms in a little straw nest and for a big centre piece a big basket planted with primroses and primulas.

Basil and Gruyère Soufflé
Serves 6

This must be the simplest soufflé I have ever made. You can make the mixture well in advance and add the egg whites at the last minute.

Set oven at 200 C, 400 F, Gas Mark 6

> 80 g butter
> 25 g basil leaves
> 6 eggs, separated
> 225 g grated gruyère
> 80 g plain flour
> 6 tablespoons single cream
> Salt, pepper and cayenne
> 1 extra egg white

Butter and flour a large soufflé dish and secure Bakewell paper around the dish to prevent the soufflé from spilling over. Remove the paper to serve. In the Magimix beat the butter with the basil, egg yolks, cheese, flour, cream, salt and pepper.

Transfer the mixture to a large bowl. Add the extra egg white to the six egg whites and beat until stiff. Gently fold into the basil mixture. Carefully pour the mixture into the soufflé dish and sprinkle with cayenne. Bake in the oven until well risen, golden and firm - about 35 minutes. Do not open the door to peep until after 25 minutes. Serve immediately.

Sardines Napolitana
Serves 6

Set oven at 200 C, 400 F, Gas Mark 6

900 g fresh sardines
2 tablespoons virgin olive oil
Salt and black pepper
2 tablespoons chopped parsley
2 cloves garlic, crushed
$^1/_2$ tablespoon fresh marjoram
Pinch of cayenne pepper
2 x 450 g tins Sainsbury's chopped tomatoes and fennel
Extra olive oil

Cut the heads off the fish, gut them, rinse and dry them. Fill a deep oven proof dish with the sardines. Mix all the remaining ingredients together and spoon over the sardines. Sprinkle with a little extra olive oil and cayenne pepper and bake for 20 minutes. Serve hot or cold with French bread and salad.

Haddock, Tomato and Asparagus Pancakes

Serves 8

Set oven at 200 C, 400 F, Gas Mark 6

Pancakes
200 g flour, sieved
Salt and pepper
2 large eggs
600 ml milk
4 tablespoons sunflower oil
Extra oil

Filling
1 kg haddock fillets, skinned
150 ml white wine
1 lemon
Butter
Salt and pepper
200 g asparagus tips
250 g tomatoes, skinned
50 g butter
2 tablespoons flour
150 ml milk
150 ml double cream
4 tablespoons grated pecorino cheese
Extra butter

To make the pancakes mix the flour, salt and pepper and eggs together and gradually incorporate with the milk and oil until you have a smooth batter. Beat for a few seconds to let in the air and then leave to settle. Pass through a sieve into a good pouring bowl or jug. Spoon a ladle full of the mixture into a very hot oiled non-stick frying pan and shake into an even pancake. Turn the pancake over and then lift on to a warm plate. When all the pancakes have been made fill them with the fish mixture.

To make the filling; poach the asparagus tips until tender in boiling, salted water and drain. Deseed the tomatoes and chop up. Bake the haddock in a buttered dish with the wine, salt and pepper, a few slices of lemon and pieces of butter. Cover with foil and cook for about 15 minutes. Remove from the oven and lift off the foil. Melt the 50 g butter in a saucepan and stir in the flour and gradually beat in all the fish juices, the milk and cream until smooth. Bring to the boil. Remove from the heat and add the fish, tomatoes and asparagus. Correct seasoning and spoon the mixture into the pancakes. Arrange them in a buttered gratin dish, sprinkle with cheese, pepper and dot with butter. Bake until bubbling and browned and serve immediately.

Strawberry and Amaretti Whip
Serves 8

This pudding is absolutely divine, incredibly quick and easy, consequently it is often my first choice for a Directors' lunch or a dinner party.

500 g ripe strawberries, hulled
100 ml Crème de Cassis liqueur
600 ml double cream, whipped to soft peaks
75 g icing sugar, sieved
75 g Amaretti biscuits, crumbled

Wash and dry the strawberries and then slice them into a pretty cut glass bowl. Pour over the Cassis and mix together. Carefully fold the icing sugar and Amaretti into the cream and gently fold the cream mixture into the strawberries. Put the pudding in the deep freeze for ten minutes and then cover and keep in the fridge until needed.

USEFUL IDEAS AND RECIPES FOR LEFTOVERS

Do you ever have that sinking feeling after Christmas as you look at all the leftovers? Tons of turkey, ham, stilton, cranberries and mincemeat! Here are a few ideas of what to do with them. In fact the recipes are so good that I often make these dishes for supper or lunch parties at other times of the year.

We call it 'Ragoût Economique'!

Turkey, Stilton and Leek Flan
Serves 6 - 8

This is such an excellent way of using up Christmas leftovers and makes a particularly good lunch or supper dish with baked potatoes and salad.

Set oven at 190 C, 375 F, Gas Mark 5

> 500 g packet fresh shortcrust pastry
> 500 g turkey meat
> 225 g stilton, crumbled
> 675 g leeks, trimmed
> 50 g butter
> 200 ml cream
> Salt, pepper and nutmeg
> 3 eggs
> Cayenne pepper and a few dots of butter

Roll out the pastry and line a large greased and floured quiche dish and refrigerate. In a small bowl beat the eggs and cream together. Chop up the turkey meat and mix with the stilton on a plate. Finely slice the leeks and cook slowly in butter until soft. Season them with salt, pepper and nutmeg and remove from the heat. Add the egg mixture, the turkey and cheese to the leeks and mix well. Fill the pastry case with this mixture and dot with butter and cayenne pepper. Bake for 35 minutes until golden brown and firm, serve warm.

Leftover Ham in Carbonara Sauce

Serves 4

I came across this marvellous idea when I was staying with Lady Tomkins, the great thing is that you can make as big a quantity as you like by buying more sauce.

Set oven at 190 C, 375 F, Gas Mark 5

350 g tub of Marks and Spencer's Carbonara Sauce
Slices of ham
Fresh black pepper
A little butter

Carve the ham and lay the slices in a buttered oven proof dish. Spread the sauce over, sprinkle with black pepper and bake in the oven for five minutes until bubbling.

Penne with Ham and Marscapone

Serves 6

I love pasta of any kind and this is my favourite recipe. Delicious with a good salad as a main course or as a smaller portion as a starter.

500 g pasta penne rigate
Salt and black pepper
350 g chopped lean ham
50 g butter
50 g grated Parmesan cheese
250 g Marscapone cream cheese

Cook the pasta in salted boiling water. Drain and mix with the butter, salt and pepper in a huge bowl. Add the ham and Parmesan. Dot the Marscapone all over and toss the pasta. Serve immediately.

Apple and Cranberry Crumble
Serves 8

A delicious change from the traditional blackberry and apple crumble. It is excellent with crème chantilly (page 61).

Set oven at 200 C, 400F, Gas Mark 6

> 340 g fresh/frozen Ocean Spray cranberries
> 8 tablespoons white sugar
> 1.6 kg cooking apples
> 1 lemon squeezed
> 1 teaspoon allspice
> 35 g butter
>
> *Crumble*
> 100 g butter
> 225 g plain flour
> 225 g sugar
> brown sugar and ground cinnamon

This recipe looks huge before cooking but shrinks during baking so choose a large oven proof dish. Put all the cranberries in the bottom and sprinkle with four tablespoons of sugar. Peel and core the apples and slice on to the cranberries. Pour the lemon juice over the apples with the remaining sugar, sprinkle with allspice and dot with butter.

Now make the crumble. Put the butter, flour and sugar in the Magimix and beat for up to ten seconds. Pat this mixture firmly down on to the apples and sprinkle with brown sugar and cinnamon. Bake in the oven for 35 minutes. Turn off the oven and leave there until ready to serve.

Mincemeat Pudding and Brandy Sauce
Serves 8

The brandy sauce is very alcoholic, but you can always add a little extra orange juice and a little less brandy if this pudding is going to be served at a family lunch or dinner.

> 450 g luxury mincemeat
> 225 g plain flour
> 3 level teaspoons baking powder
> 150 g dark brown sugar
> 150 g softened butter
> 3 large eggs
> 50 g glacé cherries, halved
> 50 g walnuts, halved
> $1/4$ teaspoon grated nutmeg
> 1 $1/2$ teaspoons mixed spice

Serve with Brandy Sauce (page 163).

Grease a large pudding basin with butter. Bring a little water to boil in a saucepan big enough to hold the pudding basin.

In a large bowl mix the mincemeat, cherries, walnuts and spices. Beat the sugar and butter together until light and fluffy, add the eggs, flour and baking powder and mix briefly. Scrape out the mixture and stir into the mincemeat. Spoon this into the pudding basin. Cover with a piece of greaseproof paper leaving plenty of room for expansion and secure with string.

Place the basin over boiling water and steam for two hours until the sponge is firm and springy. Make the brandy sauce and then turn the pudding on to a warm dish and serve with the sauce.

INDEX FOR RECIPES

*Extra Quick and Easy

Recipes for Drinks Parties

Recipes for Vegetables and Salads

Recipes for Starters

Recipes for Fish

Recipes for Poultry and Game

Recipes for Meat

Recipes for Puddings